A Doubter's Guide
to Heaven

A Doubter's Guide to

HEAVEN

Walking a Path
From Doubt to Trust

TERRY GILES

ABINGDON PRESS / Nashville

A DOUBTER'S GUIDE TO HEAVEN
WALKING A PATH FROM DOUBT TO TRUST

This book is printed on acid-free, elemental chlorine-free paper.

ISBN-13: 978-0-687-64214-4

07 08 09 10 11 12 13 14 15 16—10 9 8 7 6 5 4 3 2 1
MANUFACTURED IN THE UNITED STATES OF AMERICA

In honor of the healers among us

Contents

Preface / 9
Acknowledgments / 13

PART 1: A DOUBT EXPRESSED
 1. The Crisis: A Journey Begins / 17
 2. Do I Have a Future? / 21
 3. A Map for the Journey / 27
 4. God Tucked Me In / 39
 5. Moriah / 47
 6. A Good God? / 55

PART 2: A FORMING RESOLUTION
 7. A Vision of Hope in the Wisdom Literature / 63
 8. A Vision of Hope in the Psalms / 77
 9. A Vision of Hope in the Torah / 93

PART 3: THE JOURNEY ON
 10. Heaven Is Where You Are / 113
 11. Neither Here nor There / 119
 12. I Looked Through the Keyhole / 127
 13. A Search for a Role Model / 131

Epilogue / 147
Select Bibliography / 149
Discussion Guide / 151

PREFACE

A *DOUBTER'S GUIDE TO HEAVEN*: As the title
suggests, this book is an attempt to honestly address questions and doubts about the afterlife—at least as articulated within the Christian tradition. I'm interested in finding out about heaven and in resolving my own doubts about what might lie beyond the grave. As you will soon discover, my interest is not idle but perhaps the most important journey I have ever been on.

The word *doubter* is chosen intentionally. I am not a skeptic—although doubt and skepticism often overlap. A skeptic has no particular investment in the outcome of the issue. A doubter, though, is an altogether different matter. As a doubter, I admit I desperately want heaven to exist. It's just that I have some very real and lingering questions that have attacked the confidence I once thought was mine. My own desperate intensity is echoed in the Gospel of Mark in the cry of the father seeking, from Jesus, his son's rescue, "Immediately, the father of the child cried out and said, 'I believe; help my unbelief!' " (Mark 9:24).

The father's honesty and total transparency is something I have long admired. But now, I understand his desperateness as well. For just like this man, whose cry has become immortalized in the pages of the Bible, I too was confronted by the prospect of loss of someone I love very much; and it was in the face of that loss that I discovered my own doubt. At exactly the wrong time and in the worst of circumstances, my doubts overtook me. They came to me in a moment of crisis and shook me very deeply. It was a disturbing realization that left me in a place where I did not want to stay. And so I began a journey. I began a quest in an effort to resolve this immediate crisis. But gradually, it dawned on me that my journey has been, in no small measure, a result of the fact that the world around us is changing; and I came to realize that the way in which I had articulated my faith would no longer suffice. The result is a doubter's guide.

This book is intensely personal. For that I make no apology, but neither do I find in that fact anything particularly commendable. You are about to read a record of my journey that began in a moment of catastrophe and took me to unexpected places of discovery, including both doubt and faith. As I have journeyed, I've found that my experience of crisis is not at all unique. Many, many other people have been down the same path that I now tread. And just as others have preceded me down this path, many others will follow. It is my hope that some of what is written here may be of assistance to those walking this dark trail.

There are some things that you ought to know before you make a decision to accompany me any farther down this path of doubt. The first thing you should know is how very important I consider this quest. It seems to me that what we are about here in the pages of this book is one of the most important concerns in all of life and human experience. If there is anything at all to heaven, nirvana, the afterlife, or whatever else we might call it, the whole notion of life after death is the most important consideration in all the world. It only makes sense. If all eternity awaits us, it far outweighs in value those seemingly important issues that preoccupy us and fill our day-to-day experiences. What color to paint the house, or wondering if I'll get that promotion at work, or thinking about what kind of car to buy simply do not, in comparison, seem so important. It's not that all these other things don't matter or that they are not worth thinking about, but it's just that they pale in significance when placed alongside the alternatives of life or oblivion that confront us by the grave. And it's inescapable. Try as we might, none of us—nor any of those we love—will escape the reality of death. Given the importance of what is at stake, I want to be as certain of heaven as I am of my own name. I will settle for nothing less.

The second thing you, as a reader, ought to know is that I am conducting my quest largely within the context of the Christian tradition. That says nothing, good or bad, about other religious traditions. This book is not about the value of comparative religious traditions, and I really don't have anything to say about those other traditions. I grew up in a Christian home, went to a Christian college, and even completed a couple of graduate degrees at a Christian seminary. To boot, I teach the Bible for a living at a Christian university. Yet, for all that, I've discovered that I'm a doubter. All those things that I thought I knew about heaven left me hollow and bewildered when faced with my own oblivion, and more so with the prospect of the oblivion that might await someone I love very much.

And so my quest has led me back to the foundations. My doubts encompassed the reliability of the Bible (and so simply quoting Bible verses will not do), the credibility of religious experience (I'm not at all interested in wish fulfillment), and the integrity of professional religious people. All of this is simply to say that if you are looking for a book that presents nicely-packaged theological or religious details about heaven, you need to keep looking—this is not that book. This is not a feel-good book of sermons or anecdotes. There are parts of this book that I find uncomfortable, if not downright painful. Yet, I've not tried to be sensational, but simply honest. Like any journey, some of the pathway is pleasant and the view magnificent. Other parts of the trek are nothing short of hard work that makes you question the wisdom of taking another step. Both are to be found in the following pages. This book is a journey of doubt and a pilgrimage toward the resolution or acceptance of those doubts.

Finally, as a reader you ought to know that this is my story. I do not expect you to agree with everything I've written; I don't see how you could. My hope is that through this book you will engage in a conversation. I have concluded over the years that none of us journeys quite the same. Some of my experiences and lessons learned will resonate with you, and some will not. Some of what is included in these pages may provide a way of looking at things that will spur you on to your own resolution of doubts. What I can promise is this: If you are a doubter, you are not alone; and I invite you to join me on a journey of discovery—a doubter's guide to heaven.

—Terry Giles

ACKNOWLEDGMENTS

I WOULD LIKE TO TAKE this opportunity to acknowledge the contributions of two very special people. The illustrations in this book are the work of William J. Doan. Bill and I have walked many paths together, and his friendship is a source of great pride to me. Also, I would like to express my deepest gratitude to Cheryl, my wife. Her courage and honesty are great inspirations, and she is the purest reflection of joy that I have ever seen. I could ask for no better partner.

PART 1:

A DOUBT EXPRESSED

1

THE CRISIS: A JOURNEY BEGINS

IT WAS SUPPOSED TO BE a simple procedure. We checked into the hospital for a quick half-hour test, expecting to be back out in time for a bite of lunch. And so I was totally unprepared for what followed. My wife, Cheryl, was wheeled from the procedure room back to the hospital room where I waited for her. She was still groggy and more than a little woozy from the anesthetic used for her routine test. All seemed normal and light. I remember that the sun was shining on a layer of newly fallen snow. All of that was to change very, very quickly.

A few moments later, a man whom I had never met entered the room. He stuck out his hand for me to shake and simply said, "Hello, I'm the doctor who did your wife's procedure. Your wife has cancer." It was matter-of-fact, yet very surreal. He went on to explain something about my wife's condition, but I didn't hear any of it. My bewilderment must have been written all over my face, for after a few minutes he simply stopped his explanation and asked, "Do you understand what I'm saying to you?" And no. No, I didn't. In less time than it took for you to read these sentences, my life had turned upside down. You need to understand, my wife is the most important and best part of my life. And now she has cancer! How can that be understandable at all? It makes no sense.

With my wife still sleeping and blissfully unaware of the storm now brewing all around her, I left the room and walked down the hall. I came to a quiet place and stood before a plate-glass window looking out onto a small court-yard covered in fresh, white snow. Looking back, I'm not sure now what I was searching for: solitude—no, not really; comfort—yes; a place to cry—most definitely. But most of all I was looking for answers. I'm not sure you can really under-stand that moment unless you've been there yourself; but I knew then and there, just as clearly as I now know that I'm sitting in front of my computer, that I was beginning a quest. I wanted answers—not about the medical details and treat-ments that were going to come; I wanted answers about this ugly specter of death. And the stakes were enormously high.

I'm not sure how long I stood before that window—it could only have been a few minutes—when my stomach began to knot as I realized I needed to tell her. Somehow or other, I needed to tell my wife that she has cancer. *How am I going to do that?* Even now the terror of that moment is fresh, and that hideous feeling in the pit of my stomach returns.

I made my way back to the room and sat beside her bed. We were alone. As is typical with her, she woke with a smile, turned toward me, and stretched out her hand to touch the side of my face. I don't know why, but the first thought that came to my mind was simply, *Don't let her be alone.* And so I said to her, "We're together. I love you very much. We have cancer." And then we hugged.

Although deep down I knew, and I'm certain our doctor had no doubt, still, we were instructed not to jump to any conclusions. A biopsy was taken, and the results would be available later in the week.

The only thing I remember about that week is how I dreaded that phone call. I would jump anytime the phone rang, and my pulse would race if the light on the answering machine was flashing. When the call finally did come, it was over in less than two minutes. Our doctor began by simply saying, "I've been doing this for over twenty-five years, and these calls never get any easier. The biopsy is positive. I would like to see you and your wife in my office first thing on Monday morning." And it was over. Just like that. So brief. So simple. Yet, so final. Our lives had been changed that week, and there would be no going back.

My wife was at work, expecting me to pick her up in about half an hour. And now I had to tell her again. But no words were needed. She opened the door, slid into the car next to me, and knew. I didn't say a word—I couldn't, really—but the look on my face must have told her all she wanted to know. We hugged again, and she kissed away my tears. Imagine that! Her biopsy results came back positive, and she was kissing away my tears! We had cancer, and our journey had just begun.

The journey that began that winter day has taken me into a far and lonely place. Certainly, there have been more visits to doctors' offices, hospitals, and emergency rooms than I can recall. But in addition, that winter day began a spiritual journey for me that was as unexpected but no less real than the cancer. Suddenly, everything I thought I ever knew or believed about God, the spiritual life, and eternity was up for grabs. I no longer had time for speculation or idle chat about heaven. I wanted to know the truth about the most important thing in the entire world to me. I wanted to know the truth about my wife's eternal destiny. I wanted hope—no—I *needed* hope. And so the journey began.

2

DO I HAVE A FUTURE?

THE DIAGNOSIS OF A SERIOUS illness can change the way you think. It has for me. Some things have become a whole lot less important, while other issues now have an air of immediacy about them. One of the things that has grown steadily in importance for me is conversation. Not just the frivolous and silly times, although even those conversations are much more fun than they used to be. But the serious, personal conversations with people who are close to me—these too have become precious, like cool water on a hot day. This chapter is about a couple of those conversations.

The stillness of night has a way of bringing out the deepest and most personal of thoughts. Some of the most meaningful and most disturbing conversations I've ever had have taken place at the end of the day. Often my wife and I lie in bed and talk to each other, cherishing the closeness, before we drift off to sleep. During those times, deep thoughts surface bold and raw, without any guise or cover that they might be forced to assume during the daylight hours. Often, and particularly right after her diagnosis of cancer, our conversations would turn to remembering times shared with the kids, or funny little episodes and life experiences we'd had, or places we had been. Sometimes one or the other of us would cry if the burden we shared became just too much. And then we wouldn't talk at all, we'd just hold each other and try to live in that very precious but fleeting present moment.

It was during one of those late-night conversations that my quest really took shape. We both were feeling a bit pensive, and so the words were few and whispered. Our thoughts gradually centered on how blessed we each felt to be married to our best friend, when what had been troubling my wife finally found expression. In the quietness of that dark room, she simply asked: "Do I have a future?" Her question literally took my breath away. I can still remember the chill running down my back as the full import of her statement sank in. She was asking more than if she would survive the cancer; she wanted to know if, in either life or death, a future was waiting for her. And I determined that I had to find out.

That question, "Do I have a future?" framed the issue very well. For me, the options were either heaven or oblivion, and oblivion was an unthinkable prospect. Yet, my repulsion at the thought of this cherished person simply vanishing into nothingness was not sufficient to rule out the possibility. I had to know, and that meant a careful examination of what I thought I knew of heaven, and a reassessment of my commitment to it. I needed to answer my wife's question as honestly as I could, and so my quest began.

To answer her question, both possibilities, heaven and oblivion (there seems to me to be very little difference between hell and oblivion—both can be summed as "no future"), deserved equal examination. Oblivion, however, is simply the absence of everything, and so the burden of the quest fell to heaven. If my wife had a future, that one word stood for all that future would hold, and so I began to find out about heaven.

My quest continued in a second conversation. I am a member of the Society of Biblical Literature, the professional academic society for biblical studies. Each year a national conference of the society is held, in coordination with the

American Academy of Religion, which draws thousands of conference participants and attendees. Scholarly papers are presented, and topics of every conceivable sort are discussed. It's a wonderfully exciting event and a good opportunity to meet up with old friends. My conversation was with one such friend. I'll refer to him as Jim.

Jim and I have been friends since seminary days. He was several years ahead of me in school and actually taught one of the classes I took on historical theology. Since those days, now almost 20 years ago, we have kept in touch both through chance and planned meetings at the national conference. Jim was enthralled by systematic and historical theology, while biblical studies captured my imagination. He had gone on to teach at a nationally-recognized seminary and graduate school; while I found my niche opening the Bible to undergrads, particularly those who have never read it before. I had just finished listening to the presentation of a paper at the national conference, and as I rode the escalator down to the lobby of this fantastically-huge hotel, I saw Jim standing next to a planter, and I walked over to greet him. We hugged, purchased a couple of cups of coffee, and sat down to talk. After the usual pleasantries about how the conference was going, our conversation took a decidedly different turn.

Jim had just been contracted by a well-known publishing house to write a book on eschatology—that is, future events. He was as yet unaware of the reason for my special interest in the topic, but I told him I was very eager to learn and asked him to explain the project to me. Jim began by roughly outlining the book, and he explained the different rational systems that he would use to describe future events. He conducted a mini-debate on the fine points of difference between post-tribulationalism and pre-tribulationalism (two schemes that offer different explanations of the expected order of events when Jesus Christ returns). Jim went on to talk about dispensationalism and modified dispensationalism (again, two schemes often used to describe the future). As he talked, a strange thing began happening to me: The more Jim talked, the angrier I became, until finally I interrupted him by blurting out, "Bulls—t!"

I rarely swear, and I don't think Jim had ever heard a word like that come from me; so it's understandable that his jaw went slack and he just sat there dumbfounded. I went on to explain. I said to him, "Jim, my wife [whom he knows quite well] has cancer, and frankly I don't have time for this anymore." I went on to tell him about my quest and the search for an answer to my wife's question, "Do I have a future?" Then I said to him, "Unless your book answers that question, it isn't worth the paper it's written on."

When I finally finished my tirade, I noticed that people sitting next to us were beginning to leave, and so we sat in silence. We both just sat there, and then tears began flowing down Jim's face. What I didn't know was that Jim had lost his mother earlier that same year, and his grief was still very sharp. He told me about her death and the funeral, and then we both cried, sometimes with his hand on my arm, sometimes with my hand on his.

We both grieved, but oddly the reason for our grief began to shift. As we talked, I told him how hollow I felt, and how I felt that much of my theological and religious training had left me without answers at the most crucial time in my life. Jim nodded his agreement and added his disappointment with the condition of his own work, suggesting that his theological writing was an effort at avoiding the deep issues of life rather than answering them.

It was that last point Jim made that has stuck with me: *How much of the religious rhetoric surrounding heaven is, in reality, an effort to avoid the question rather than answer it? Does heaven really exist? How do we know the truthfulness of so much we claim?*

My doubts began to form. Not simply doubts about a subject (heaven) that could be answered by accessing more information—you know, reading another book or listening to another taped sermon. Nor could they be answered by confessing my sin in prayer. No, my doubts quickly assumed a very foundational character. They were not simply the result of a lack of knowledge about heaven, but rather they included sincere and serious questions about the validity of those *sources* of knowledge. How can I be certain that the sources upon which I have relied are, in fact, worthy of my trust? Is guidance available, and can a reliable guide be found?

Is there a map for the journey?

3

A MAP FOR THE JOURNEY

YOGI BERRA IS FAMOUS FOR reportedly advising, "When you come to a fork in the road—take it" (also the title of a book by Berra; Hyperion, 2001). I can identify with this uncertainty and sense of confusion. In the quest for heaven there are many forks in the road, and precious few signposts directing the way.

As I have discovered, my quest for heaven has also included a crisis of faith. Whenever you lose confidence in things you thought you knew or trusted in, you are forced to reconsider the whole process by which knowledge is to be had. On our journey of discovery, how will we know which fork in the road to take? When it comes to our search for heaven, what will be our guide? How will we know the answers to questions that are going to be asked? For many, the basis for determining valid knowledge about heaven, or spirituality at all for that matter, is the real crux. Doubters are, first and foremost, questioners of the status quo. We need a map. So, in this chapter we are going to try to fix a manner for determining valid knowledge about heaven.

Historically, there have been three or four main sources of information by which Christians, or those somehow identifying with Christianity, have tried to make determinations about heaven, eternity, and the spiritual realm. In one form or another, religious authorities, or the Bible, or a remarkable experience, all coupled with a sense of reasonableness, have served as the foundation for knowledge about heaven. We have turned to favorite verses from the Bible (often 1 Corinthians 15), or we have sought out persuasive and popular preachers and the endless stream of books that they produce in order to satisfy our questions and concerns about eternity. Yet for many of us, a great many of us, the foundations have begun to crumble.

Many have sought refuge in a church tradition or authority. It only makes sense. If you want to know what's wrong with the brakes on your car, you go to someone who repairs brakes—you go to an authority. So if you want to know about heaven, go ask somebody who makes their living knowing about such things. But for many doubters, this method no longer works. And it no longer works for two reasons.

First, there are simply too many competing and contradictory claims made by religious leaders. The credibility of the whole lot suffers when no consensus can be reached on the seemingly most fundamental and important matters. In the competition for parishioners, it is often the new and exciting that is presented as religious truth. That's what draws crowds and builds buildings. But this spirit of religious entrepreneurship suffers from a lack of accountability. Unlike medical or legal professionals who may be held accountable for the advice they dispense, there is no similar mechanism for testing the ultimate-truth claims of religious professionals. And so, just about anything goes.

What this means for us doubters is that much of what is currently being said about heaven we reject, because it simply doesn't make sense. It all seems to be subject to an ulterior agenda on the part of the speaker. I can still remember being amazed while listening to a sermon in which the preacher was explaining that scientists had discovered an enormous and cubical object deep within our galaxy that was hurtling toward Earth at tremendous speeds. The preacher spoke with great passion, convinced that astronomers actually had discovered heaven, and that this cosmic entity would soon be here. What amazed me was not that the preacher had so constructed his theory of heaven, but that he had done so at the height of the popularity of *Star Trek: The Next Generation*. He seemed to be totally unaware that his description of heaven exactly matched the design of the Borg mother ship! Maybe, as the Borg mechanical monsters were fond of saying, "resistance is futile"; I certainly felt like giving up.

The second reason for the loss of credibility among religious voices is that the advice isn't accompanied by a sense of sincerity or integrity. When you go to the garage for repairs to your car, it's easy to figure out whether the mechanic knows how to fix brakes: You try them out, preferably with the mechanic sitting in the car next to you. If the mechanic refuses to go for a test-drive after repairing the brakes, that's a pretty good sign that you shouldn't get into the car either. The same applies to religious authorities and the expertise they claim. For sure, we can't ask them to accompany us on a visit to heaven in order to test out the truthfulness of their directions, but we can look at how committed they are to the advice they give to others. We can observe whether they live according to what they preach. And that is exactly where many religious figures have lost their credibility—especially for doubters.

I can be criticized for being extremely judgmental in what I'm about to write; so be it. Heaven is an important issue, and it seems to me that we all ought to be very judgmental about persons who presume to make statements designed to affect our eternal afterlife. I am very careful and judgmental about whom I choose to work on the brakes of my car; how can I be less so toward those who claim to speak for God about eternity? What bothered me, and still does, about many of the religious people in my life is that I would be hard-pressed to prove that they really believe what they are saying. I'm not trying to say that they are being intentionally dishonest by what they're saying; but in my experience, rarely does the lifestyle of the speaker affirm what is said.

Soon after the diagnosis of cancer, when my quest to discover the reality of heaven began, I sought a role model who might guide me on my way. I wanted to find a person whose conduct of life visibly demonstrated a belief in heaven. I searched among religious professionals and became bitterly disappointed. I could not find one. I've come to discover that many share my disappointment, and this disappointment has led to the growing crisis of credibility. Let me see if I can illustrate what I mean.

Over a period of 18 months I closely watched our local newspaper as well as several papers with national and international audiences, and it was always the same. When representatives from religious organizations, or other religious authorities and spokespersons, were being interviewed, the topic of conversation seemed to inevitably revolve around efforts expended in trying to keep each other out of jail by dodging sex crimes, or the announcement of a new building program or capital campaign to buy new property. These sorts of things seem to be what preoccupy many religious establishments. Even when the person interviewed was given free reign to discuss whatever was on their mind—the topic of heaven never came up. Seemingly, heaven isn't what these religious authorities are concerned about.

I recently heard a sermon that only enhanced my cynicism. A church was beginning a capital campaign in order to raise money to fund the construction of a bigger building and to buy more property. The pastor of this church decided to deliver a sermon on heaven as a way of kicking off the campaign. He chose Matthew 6:19-21 as his preaching text. This text reads: "Do not store up for yourselves treasures on earth, where moth and rust consume and where thieves break in and steal; but store up for yourselves treasures in heaven, where neither moth nor rust consumes and where thieves do not break in and steal. For where your treasure is, there your heart will be also" (NRSV).

The preacher spoke eloquently about the permanence of the eternal state, especially when compared to the brief time that we spend in this life. This awareness of the brevity of life led to the main point of the sermon, that people ought to give money to the church's capital campaign, for in so doing they were building up a bank account in heaven. Somehow, according to him, placing money in the building fund amounted to making a deposit of like funds in heaven. (The preacher never explained why we need money in heaven, but I guess that was a topic for a different sermon.) The decision to give money to the church was simply a matter of determining the best rate of return on an investment. I came away thinking that there must be more. Heaven must be more than a marketing ploy for raising money.

The second foundation that many have used in making judgments about heaven is the Bible. To be sure, there are many, many statements about heaven made in the books of the Bible; but the problem runs much deeper. Quoting a favorite Bible verse to answer a question about heaven only makes sense if first it is established that the Bible gives reliable information on the topic—and for many, including doubters, this is no longer a given. Serious questions currently are on the table concerning the authenticity of the books of the Bible; the reliability of the selection process by which only *some* ancient writings were included in the Bible while others were not; and the continued value of the biblical worldview, now so far removed from that of our own space and time. How can we be certain that the Bible is an accurate and reliable guide? And whose interpretation of the Bible should guide our quest? And why stop at the Bible? Why not consult the Koran or some other sacred text?

It seems just about everybody has read *The Da Vinci Code* (Doubleday, 2003). It's a great read. This popular book is Dan Brown's fictional account of church intrigue, murder, and deceit. Part of the plot involves the "lost books" of the Bible, books that are reported to give quite a different take on the life of Jesus and the early church. This fictional and imaginative book touches on a very real problem that is once again making quite a stir in scholarly circles. It has always been a bit of a mystery why some documents from the first- and second-century church made it into the Bible, while others did not. What has become very clear in the last several years is that the early church used and circulated quite a number of scrolls and codices that are not found between the covers of a modern-day New Testament. Once again, some of those writings are being discovered by a wide public. The rub is that some of the writings cast quite a different light on the power structures of the formal church, and there is a growing realization that the maintenance of power structures set by the third- and fourth-century church authorities played a very large role in deciding which books to include in the New Testament collection. The point is, the decision about which books were to be considered the Word of God was made, at least in part, to keep some people in power and prestige, and to keep other people on the margins. This problem of understanding the formation of the Bible has been addressed by scholars from a wide range of perspectives. Some books include: *The Biblical Canon: Its Origin, Transmission, and Authority*, by Lee Martin McDonald (Hendrickson, 2007); *Beyond Belief: The Secret Gospel of Thomas*, by Elaine Pagels (Random House, 2003); *The Canon Debate*, edited by Lee Martin McDonald and James A. Sanders (Hendrickson, 2002); and *Lost Christianities: The Battles for Scripture and the Faiths We Never Knew*, by Bart D. Ehrman (Oxford University Press, 2003).

Given this small bit of political history that went in to the makeup of the New Testament, this question surely comes to the fore: *How can I trust that these small books comprising the New Testament are, in fact, God's word to me, when I know full well that those same books were subject to and*

tools of the political power struggles between church groups?
To add more confusion to the mix, I stumbled upon an old
Samaritan document that describes the kingdom of the
Nazarene (i.e., Christians) of the first couple of centuries. I
read in amazement as this Samaritan author listed the books
that he knew were used by the Nazarenes. I counted 35
"gospel books," only a few of which I recognized (*Tradition
Kept: The Literature of the Samaritans*, by Robert T. Anderson
and Terry Giles; Hendrickson, 2005; pages 259–60). Here
was an unbiased testimony of a person who had nothing to
gain or lose—someone who didn't have a vested interest in
any of the books in the New Testament—and he had come
up with a whole different list than what I am familiar with.
Early Christians used different books than I now use, and
they too were convinced that they were reading God's Word.
I determined that no longer would the old argument work
that says I can trust the books of the Bible *because* they are
Bible; there must be more to the trustworthiness of the Bible
than a self-affirming, circular argument.

Whether it's advice given by a religious person or a sacred
book, the problem is the same: How can we ascertain its reliability? How will we know which fork in the road to take?
This book isn't the place to try to answer all those questions
of reliability, but I am going to suggest to you a "map" that
may be of use on our journey. This map of sorts is not orig-
inal to me, but rather was first brought to my attention by
the words of Jesus found in one of the Gospel books of the
Bible. Now, given what I've just said about the reliability of
the Bible and other religious sources, you might wonder, isn't
it rather odd now for me to be quoting a verse from the
Bible? Yes, but hear me out. When Jesus was asked about the
reliability of religious teaching of the prophets of his day, he
responded quite simply and straightforwardly, "You will
know them by their fruits. Are grapes gathered from thorns,
or figs from thistles? In the same way, every good tree bears

good fruit, but the bad tree bears bad fruit. ... Thus you will know them by their fruits" (Matthew 7:16-17, 20, NRSV). "By their fruits you will know them." Whether the authority in question is a person or a book, the advice given or beliefs recommended ought to have positive results—good fruit. And it is this test of positive results that I believe completes or holds accountable the sources from which we may gather information. I don't recommend this standard to you because it is in the Bible, nor even because it claims to come from Jesus. I recommend it to you because I think it works—at least, it works for doubters. I have found that some claims about heaven simply ring true, regardless of the source (be it through an experience, from some authority such as the church or the Bible, or even if it just "makes sense"). They touch me deeply and have a profoundly positive effect on me. Such statements or convictions about heaven produce good fruit, and in an almost intuitive fashion I know they are true. There is a resonance deep within that confirms the truthfulness of a statement or belief.

And so I decided to apply the standard developed by Jesus. When asked how to distinguish the true from the false among people who present themselves as God's representatives, Jesus replied that it is by their fruits you will know them. If this test works for people, it ought to work for books, too. I have determined that at least as far as information about heaven is concerned—I will put it to the test. I will accept it as authoritative if it strikes me on a deep level as true, if the Word of God is powerful and active (see Hebrews 4:12); and then I will put it to the test and see.

Let me be quick to say that I am not advocating heaven as wish fulfillment; in other words, I am not saying that you or I can believe things about the afterlife to be true simply because we *want* them to be so. I frankly have no time for that sort of reasoning, and I would not recommend such a thing to you. And this is not what I mean at all when I suggest that we allow a deep resonance to help guide us along our way. No, what I have in mind is a deep sense of functionality. If the Creator has embedded within us a vague awareness of the eternal—as the writer of Ecclesiastes 3:11 believed, "He has made everything suitable for its time; moreover he has put a sense of past and future into their minds"—then it may be that our beliefs about the eternal can either be in concert or in disharmony with that deeply-embedded awareness (NRSV). Beliefs and convictions that are in concert with this embedded awareness make us more functional than do attempts to live with perceptions and behaviors that are not. We live with this sort of thing all the time. The clean and sweet mountain air is more appealing than city smog because we function better without inhaling a multitude of pollutants. Likewise, most of us can identify the optimum number of hours of sleep our bodies need each night to function properly. A longing for the eternal is no more a symptom of wish fulfillment than is the desire for clean air, sufficient rest, or healthy food. We simply function better when we are mindful of the way we were made. Giving adequate attention to what enables us to function well isn't engaging in fantasy; it simply makes sense.

This deeply-embedded drive or desire has been variously described over the years. C. S. Lewis calls it "joy." He writes that all our experiences of joy are but a shadow or a taste. They are partial confirmations of the greater substance that is the real object of our joy. Lewis means that the encounters we have with people or things in which we find joy are joyful because at some deep level they awaken our delight in the source of all joy—God himself (*Surprised by Joy: The Shape of My Early Life*; Harcourt Brace Jovanovich, 1955; pages 222–29; *The Problem of Pain*, fourth edition; Fontana Books, 1962; pages 134–36). Blaise Pascal likens this awakening to a God-shaped vacuum deep inside that calls us to search for its ultimate fulfillment (*Pensées/The Provincial Letters*, translated by W. F. Trotter and Thomas M'Crie; Modern Library, 1941; pages 134–35). Likewise, Augustine refers to this as a restlessness, satisfied only in God (*The Confessions of Saint Augustine*, translated by John K. Ryan; Doubleday, 1960; page 43). Søren Kierkegaard calls this deep awareness "essential truth" (*A Kierkegaard Anthology*, edited by Robert Bretall; Modern Library, 1946; page 218). By that term, he means a knowledge that comes alive when experienced and is, in turn, essential for understanding that experience.

Not all have looked upon this longing as a positive condition. Sigmund Freud has a much less charitable view. He was convinced that this deep drive or desire is a universal human neurosis to be dispelled and driven from us (*The Standard Edition of the Complete Psychological Works of Sigmund Freud*, Vol. 21, translated by James Strachey; Hogarth Press, 1961; page 43). Martin Heidegger calls it a sign of inauthenticity (*Being and Time*, translated by John Macquarrie and Edward Robinson; Harper and Row, 1962; pages 306–09). But all agree, for good or ill, that this deep drive is within us all. The drive is there—nothing to be done about that. The matter before us is what to do with the drive for the eternal that is buried deep within each of us.

Lewis's assessment of the drive, the joy, leads us back to the idea of functionality. He likens his conviction of heaven to a sunbeam streaming into a darkened room. As long as he stood alongside the beam of light, it was an anomaly that did little to change the gloom and shadow within the room. The light mattered little at all. If, however, he stood in the beam of light and looked out the window toward the source of the light, a whole new world, bright and colorful, came into view. (This idea is expressed in a wonderful story in one of the last chapters of *The Last Battle*, in *The Complete Chronicles of Narnia*, by C. S. Lewis; HarperCollins, 1998; pages 506–11.)

This is how it is with heaven. I don't believe in heaven because I see it so clearly, but because by believing in heaven everything else becomes much easier to see. My quest for heaven is making me more functional. And it is this test that I now recommend to you. Whatever the source of the information, it is incomplete unless it resonates within you— unless you are seeing more clearly and becoming more functional.

In the pages that follow, I am going to do my best to describe some of my discoveries of heaven that have most resonated within me. They will not all be of one kind. Some of the discoveries were the result of special moments of experience, others the product of information gleaned from the Bible, and still others came as unexpected encounters in prayer. These discoveries have helped me become more functional and to see the world around me a bit more clearly. Some of these discoveries, I hope, will do the same for you.

But here's the catch: There is no substitute for the journey. Neither I, nor anyone else, can take the journey for you; and the paths we take may not be exactly the same. Your journey will be distinctly yours. As you read, however, we will journey together, and I will be glad for the company.

4

GOD TUCKED ME IN

IN THE LAST CHAPTER, I argued that the most meaningful guidance about heaven is the result of an intersection
at which information we receive, from a variety of possible
sources, resonates deeply within us. The resultant confluence
of this information and resonance provides a firm foundation
for belief or conviction. This chapter is about one of those
very special intersections. It has touched me deeply and
seems like a good place to start our journey.

The day of Cher's surgery to treat her cancer was one of
the most difficult days I have ever experienced. The hospital
at which the surgery was scheduled is about 150 miles from
our home. We were instructed to register at the hospital at
6:00 A.M. The night before the surgery, we set the alarm for
3:00 A.M. and tried to get at least a few hours of sleep. My
wife can sleep in just about any circumstances, and she did
that night as well. I, on the other hand, tossed and turned,
was showered and up waiting for the alarm to go off.

At that time of early morning, there is very little traffic,
and so I could drive and get lost in my own thoughts at the
same time. My wife promptly fell asleep again in the car. The
trip to the hospital was uneventful and much too brief.

Registration went smoothly, and in due time we were sent
to the family waiting room. From there, my wife was called
to make her way up to the hospital room, where we were met

by the surgeon. She was a wonderful person. Small and spry with a smile that radiated, she joined us in the room, dressed in her scrubs, with a wildly-colored bonnet over her hair. She explained that the operating room was being prepped and that we were next.

During the conversation, one of the operating personnel entered our room with news that all was now ready. Immediately, the small, spry, and friendly woman transformed into a no-nonsense, all-business, single-minded surgeon. I bent over my wife's bed, prayed with her, gave her a kiss; and down the hall they went. I remember thinking two things: First, I had a sinking feeling as the doors closed behind my wife; and second, I thought to myself, *I sure wouldn't want to get in that doctor's way right now—she means business!*

I made my way back to the family waiting room. It was a large room, apportioned with comfortable chairs, televisions, a coffee maker, and plenty of magazines. Incoming phone calls were taken by a receptionist, who would call out a family name for a member of that family to come and take the call. Those of us who were there for a long period soon discovered that there was a rhythm to the place. A phone call meant good news: Someone from the surgical team would call down to report on the good progress of the surgery, or with the news that the family could soon go up and be with the patient. When the surgery did not go well, or if there was bad news to relate, the surgeon would come in person and usher the waiting family off to a little conference room, and there try to break the news as kindly and as humanely as possible. So when the phone rang, we would all look at one another or we would look expectantly at the receptionist— each of us hoping that it would be us whose wait would end with good news, but happy for another family when they were called up to take the phone call. Likewise, when a door opened and we saw the green surgical outfit, the tension rose noticeably, knowing that someone was being called into the conference room.

Because of the hospital's distance from home, I waited alone. I spent a good deal of time observing the other families, taking hope from the good news they received, and empathizing deeply with those who were called to the conference room. But as the day wore on, I wore out. The surgery was supposed to take about four hours. But as five and then six hours marched by, the reality of all this weighed ever more heavily on me. The receptionist took special note of those of us who had been there the longest, and every so often she would engage us in conversation just to pass the time, and more, to let us know, in her own way, that she was concerned for us.

In the middle of the afternoon the phone rang, and finally, the call was for me. The voice on the other end of the phone simply said things were going well, it was taking a bit longer than they thought, they would get back to me. At first I was thrilled. I got a phone call, and not a visit! But then I remembered, *It's not over yet. We've a ways to go.*

The receptionist must have noticed the look on my face. She gently suggested that I take a break and go get something to eat. She gave me directions to the cafeteria and promised that she would send someone to notify me should any news arrive. Food was out of the question—I didn't have much of an appetite—but the walk did me wonders. When I got back, the waiting room was pretty much emptied out and everyone else gone, and I finally received another call. "Your wife is in recovery. Come on up in about half an hour." That was good news, but I think that last half hour took longer to pass than the preceding eight.

I was not at all prepared for what I saw when I went into Cher's room. Her face was swollen, a trickle of blood had dried on the corner of her mouth, and tubes seemed to surround her. My attention was riveted on my wife, and so I was surprised when a voice beside me said, "I think we got it." My wife's surgeon was standing next to me, and she went on to say, "We need to wait for the biopsies, but I think we got it." I then turned to look at the speaker and was again surprised. All of the bounce had gone out of the surgeon's step. This woman looked exhausted. Her eyes were red, her shoulders stooped, and that colorful bonnet was now all bunched up, squeezed in her left hand. I'm not a hugger. I generally shy away from that sort of thing, but I hugged her. She had visibly spent herself in care for my wife, and I was very thankful for what she had done that day.

The surgeon then explained to me that the next few hours were really important and how the hospital staff would care for my wife throughout that crucial period. Then she told me to go home. I felt as tired as she looked, so I didn't argue at all. One more kiss on my wife's forehead, and then down the elevator and out the hall.

I wish I had the right words to express the feelings I felt on the drive home. It was awful. The image of Cher's swollen face with a trickle of blood kept coming back again and again. The closer I got to home, the more I knew I had one more task before the day could finish. Earlier, I had called family and friends to give them updates on how the surgery was going, but now I had to talk to the kids. At the time, my wife and I had two children still living at home. They had had a difficult day as well. Both had tried to keep busy with all the normal things teenagers do. School, part-time jobs, homework, and supper at Grandma's had all provided for them a measure of preoccupation. But now, I needed to explain to them what had happened that day and how their mom was doing.

It was late by the time I drove into the driveway. Both kids were in bed, neither asleep. In turn, I went to each of them, sat on the side of the bed, and told them that their mom was doing fine. I lied. The words I spoke and the image I had in my memory did not at all coincide. But I figured, now is not the time—they've had long days, too. Let them sleep. So, words of comfort and reassurance, and then hugs all around would be the way this day ended for them.

I then made my way to our room. The bed was still unmade from our early morning departure. My mind was racing from the events of the day, and I could not escape that image of my wife lying in bed, swollen and bleeding. I remember flopping back onto the bed and beginning to sob. The tension was like a dam that had burst, and now there was no stopping the tears.

The next part I remember like it was yesterday. I prayed a very short prayer—one word, really. I simply said, "Help!" The response was immediate and unmistakable. In fact, what happened next is the whole reason for this chapter.

I have tried to come up with a better description to explain what happened, but I always come back to saying simply that God tucked me in. I have never felt anything like it in my life, neither before nor since. Immediately after my one-word prayer, I experienced an overwhelming sense of emotional and physical comfort and security. It was like the sort of feeling that would come when, as a young child, your mother tucked you into bed at night. And I slept soundly. "Likewise the Spirit helps us in our weakness; for we do not know how to pray as we ought, but that very Spirit intercedes with sighs too deep for words" (Romans 8:26, NRSV).

God tucked me in. Since then, I have spoken with others and have found that some, at least, have shared my experience. Some said it was like being in the arms of God or a complete sense of security. For those I found who had a similar encounter, the experience was unexpected, coming during a time of utter helplessness and providing a feeling beyond compare. No matter how hard they tried, they reported, not one could duplicate or recapture that wonderful moment.

There are several cryptic statements in the Psalms that seem to be descriptions of something close to this very special experience. Psalm 27:10 reads, "For my father and my mother have forsaken me, / but the LORD will take me up." This verse is the very culmination of a terrible expression of abandonment. Bereft of the close comfort and security of family and without hope, surrounded by terrible alternatives, God stepped in. The love, warmth, and comfort associated with parents was provided by God and experienced in a very real and tangible way. The same is found in Psalm 103:13, "As a father has compassion for his children, / so the LORD has compassion for those who fear him" (NRSV). Right at the heart and center of Psalm 103 is the image of a loving father—one who lovingly scoops up and holds his small child who has come running to him with a cut finger or a bad dream. All the child knows is that daddy will make it better. And every bit of the father's attention is riveted on that one small child who now occupies the very center of his universe.

The point is, for me at least, that this bit of information about God, gleaned from the Psalms, was joined with a remarkable experience that has resounded deeply within me. I had read those verses in the Psalms thousands of times, but it wasn't until my experience of being "tucked in" that this bit of information became functional for me. And now, that increased functionality, as we recall Jesus' remark that "by their fruits you will know them," has provided a signpost directing our quest.

Don't get me wrong; I'm not saying that all such signposts are so dramatic in nature. What is evident, however, is that the most useful and credible bits of information about the spiritual realm, life with God, or heaven are those that awaken a God-echo within us, resounding deeply within and making us more functional. It's what C. S. Lewis calls believing in heaven, and so being able to see everything else more clearly. That's how we know the information is reliable.

But now, what about the information itself? Having established some test for judging its reliability, what do these verses from the Psalms, or my experience of being "tucked in by God," tell us about heaven? There seems to be a bottom line. Whatever else might be said about heaven, this much is true: Heaven is the result of realizing that you are fixed in the center of God's attention. Or to say it another way, heaven is fully realizing the closeness of God.

To be sure, there seems to be an intensity of that experience that awaits us when the final hurdle of separation, the grave, is overcome. But apparently it is possible to catch bits and pieces of that reality now. Could that be what Jesus was talking about when he declared, "The kingdom of God is in the midst of you" (Luke 17:21)? Certainly, he never suggested that the full reality of the kingdom of God (Luke's term), or the kingdom of heaven (Matthew's term), was here and now. Jesus always gave the impression that something very big was on its way. But one of the sure proofs that heaven is out there somewhere waiting for us is the experience of tantalizing tastes of heaven *now*.

After all, that's the whole point of the discussion in Luke 17. The Pharisees have asked Jesus: How can we know or recognize the kingdom of God? What serves as a reliable signpost showing us the way? Is there evidence? It was to this kind of question that Jesus replied that the Kingdom is in the midst of us—it's an experience with God that we begin to encounter now.

> Being asked by the Pharisees when the kingdom of God was coming, he answered them, "The kingdom of God is not coming with signs to be observed; nor will they say, 'Lo, here it is!' or 'There!' for behold, the kingdom of God is in the midst of you." (Luke 17:20-21)

And that present experience, the kingdom of God "in the midst of you," is the best way of knowing that more is on the way. For some, as Jesus indicated, that experience should serve as a warning against the pursuit of a lifestyle unacceptable in the kingdom of heaven (Matthew 13:24-30, 40-43); but for others it is a source of comfort and confidence, a way of seeing all of life a bit more clearly (5:3-10, 14-16). That experience with God that allows us to see life more clearly is what will occupy us in the pages to come.

5

MORIAH

As I HAVE PROGRESSED THROUGH this journey, I have come to realize that my doubts are not centered on a *place*. The very heart of the matter is not a set of questions about a place like heaven, paradise, or whatever else you might want to call this future expectation. Nor have they been doubts about the *description* of future existence—the kinds of things a person might do, or things to see and experience—that might be available in this place we call heaven. No, in the end, my doubts come down to doubts about God. Doubts about God's goodness and approachability, at least in any manner that comes close to personal awareness, love, or concern. This is the very center of my doubt. There is no use trying to avoid it, and there is no useful way to polish it up.

Moreover, I've learned that my experience, once again, is not unique. Whether it's the fault of the manner in which religious-minded people have portrayed God, or a function of the religious reformation now sweeping across North America, or whether the fault lies with God himself, there are many, many people who have substantial misgivings about God and the goodness of God's character. There are a lot of us who think that God has some answering to do. This chapter and the next are about those misgivings.

I've concluded that my doubts have been spurred on by deep disappointment. The world in which I once lived has vanished. I mistakenly but happily believed that I lived in a world not touched by the specter of death. I had every reason to believe that things would work out and that I was somehow immune to tragedy. Even writing these sentences now makes me embarrassed at my thoughtlessness and arrogance, but I have come to conclude that there are many of us who are quite happily living with self-imposed blinders on—until, that is, these blinders get ripped from our eyes by the unexpected and uncontrollable. I had been living in a world dominated by naïve goodness (and a fair amount of selfishness) that was suddenly replaced by questions concerning the right of God to grant existence to those who never asked for this burdensome gift. My cavalier outlook on life was unexpectedly overcome by a sense of betrayal. God had betrayed me. What right does God have to grant life to people like us, only to have that life—sometimes slowly and sometimes suddenly, but always surely—seep away? Can this God be good? Is God some cosmic trickster who holds before us this wonderful gift of life only to remove it from our reach? Can this God be relied upon in any meaningful way?

While these questions must be addressed (and will be over the next several chapters), the immediate need is more basic. In the following several pages, I would like to describe a moment of resonance that, like C. S. Lewis's sunbeam in a dark room, allowed me to see the world around me just a bit more clearly. During dark days filled with questions like those just mentioned, a part of the Bible that has always been a mystery to me suddenly made sense.

Genesis 22 contains one of the most awful tales in the entire Bible. At God's direction, Abraham is led up the slopes of Mount Moriah in order to place his son, Isaac, on an altar. There, under divine order, Abraham is to put a knife to his son's throat and offer him as a sacrifice to God. Isaac's life is to end—and God is responsible. It is true that most Bible commentaries on this chapter emphasize Abraham's complete trust in God. And while Abraham's trust in God is certainly evident, I think there is much more, and the depth of the episode becomes clear only when we allow the emotional nature of the story full flight. In fact, the expression of Abraham's trust is remarkable only when paired with the horrible emotional price that was paid.

The starkness of the story accounts for its terrible nature. There is no getting God off the hook. He is responsible for the clear and present danger that now threatens Abraham's beloved son. Can you imagine the horror raging in Abraham's mind? What kind of God would do such a thing? Isaac's birth was long desired, and the story gives every indication that Isaac was dearly loved by his father, Abraham. How Abraham's heart must have broken, and how he must have hated God! Why did God need another sacrifice? Weren't the lambs and goats enough? Why did God want Isaac?

And now, why did God want my wife? Why didn't God prevent the cancer? After all, he is *God*, right? Can't God do something about this? Why does God require my wife to now be placed upon an altar at the summit of my own Moriah? For me, the clarity of the parallel was unmistakable. Just as God was solely responsible for the claim upon Isaac, so God could not elude responsibility for what was now happening to my wife. Isaac was being ripped from the care and security that Abraham could provide, and just as unquestionably, God was taking my wife, Cher, from my care.

For the first time in my life I began to feel the intensity and the terribleness of this strange story in Genesis 22. If I too was journeying up a Mount Moriah of sorts, then I can attest that every step became harder than the one before. Part of the journey's difficulty is the inherent loneliness of the path. Although friends and family offer support and comfort, Mount Moriah will admit only one at a time up its slope. Mortality's struggle with God is very personal and, I suspect, unavoidable. The story in Genesis 22 ends with a miraculous rescue in which Isaac is spared and God is vindicated—kind of.

The intensity of my wrestling cannot be overstated. Bitterness, rage, and despair all took their turns firing salvo after salvo at God. Yet, a joy of equal strength became an unexpected reply to my struggle. Later in the biblical record (2 Chronicles 3:1), Mount Moriah is identified as the mount upon which Jerusalem was built; and it is generally associated with the mount ascended by another Son and his Father years later. The long and painful trek taken by Abraham and Isaac was repeated years later by Jesus and his Father, up what was now called Mount Calvary. This time, however, there would be no rescue. There would be no ram caught in a thicket by its horns. The horror and grief from which Abraham was spared by the sudden restraining hand of an angel would rest fully on this Father, God, as he agonized over the loss of his Son.

It may sound strange, but that awful story in Genesis 22 resonated deeply within me. I came to realize that God himself has experienced and shared in my grief. He has been to Moriah before, and he has tasted the same bitter cup that was now at my lips. My joy was in this: God knows! God knows fully the depth of grief to which Abraham was only introduced. God knows, firsthand, the bitter grief I tasted as my dear loved one was placed on an altar of a different kind. My questions, doubts, rage, and bitterness were met not with a stern divine rebuke, but with empathy and understanding. My questions of "why" were never answered. Instead, I found a place to cry with Someone who had been there before.

Although I have never been a poet, I admire the way in which poems can capture so much with so few words. The following is how the sentiments of Genesis 22 worked their way into a poem for me:

It's a Long and Lonely Climb

It's a long and lonely climb up the slopes of Moriah
Like Abram of old tenderly placing Isaac on the altar,
I release you from my care to the care of God.
It's a long and lonely climb up the slopes of Moriah
I kissed your lips and said goodbye.
I watched as your bed was wheeled away.
The doors closed and the hall was empty.
It's a long and lonely climb up the slopes of Moriah
The surgeon looks so small.
Her hands once deft and sure now rub tired eyes
Her voice worn and spent
It's a long and lonely climb up the slopes of Moriah
I watch you sleep and know you're safe, hid in the hand
of God
For, he's been there before on that long and lonely climb
up the slopes of Moriah

As I look back, I realize that there have been few experiences in my life more symbolically poignant than that moment when I watched the doors close behind my wife as she was being wheeled to surgery. When those doors closed, my wife was inarguably beyond my care and in the care of someone else. Ultimately, that "someone else" was God, and at that moment my wife's question was being answered. She had asked if she had a future, and the answer was being given at that very moment. This was her future—behind those doors—and whatever happened behind those doors was outside my control. Could God be relied upon to provide for my wife what I could not? Can God be trusted?

Once I came to understand that my doubts were more about God than anything else, and once I knew that God understood my grief, I became free to ask a whole new set of questions. I discovered that my doubts were not about *heaven* at all; I discovered that through this whole experience, my images and conceptions of *God* were being broken and shattered. Cruelly, at times, it felt as though God remained just out of reach, but not out of sight. Yet, as the encounter with Genesis 22 taught me, the old image can be replaced by new and brighter images, images more lofty and real. But there was more. What a startling discovery it was to find that it was God who was breaking the old images. It was God who was taking my old and quite dysfunctional conceptions and reforming them, replacing them with something new. The Creator is the great iconoclast.

I slowly realized that my doubts were in large measure due to the fact that my old conceptions of God simply wouldn't work. Those images and conceptions were now broken and scattered, like a favorite coffee mug that had slipped from my hand, crashed, and now lay shattered on the floor. There was an inevitable sense of loss when those images of God that I had grown comfortable with were now destroyed. A vacuum had formed as the old images and thought patterns became untenable but had not yet been replaced by something better and more real. That sense of loss is the dark side of doubt, but it's not the only side. My encounter with Genesis 22 was the beginning of the dawning realization that for too long my gaze had been transfixed by that old image of God that, like an old mug broken on the floor, was now nothing more than worthless pieces and splinters. And as with the loss of anything important and of value, when my old conception of God and the world around me was shattered, it was accompanied by grief, anger, and disappointment. It wasn't until I began to look up when in prayer and in conversation with friends, and to meditate on the small sentences in the Bible, that a new vision began to take shape.

And this may be the best part. Could it be that the shattering of my old image of God is the greatest evidence for God's presence? For how could the false and temporary be so recognized if not for the presence of what is more real and permanent? How could my image of God be recognized as broken if not for the sudden presence of something more real, something beyond my control and beyond my creation? The old dysfunction had given way to something more functional—something closer to what I was created for. It is for good reason that the first of the Ten Commandments is "You shall have no other gods before me" (Exodus 20:3). It's for our benefit. We are created to function best when dependent upon the Creator. My encounter with Genesis 22 led me to recognize that my doubts stemmed from the inadequacy of my image of God. I now realized that whatever future my wife might have, it would be with the God of Genesis 22; and I was now free to discover this God. Through this lengthy series of experiences, a verse from the Book of Proverbs came to surface again and again in my thinking. Proverbs 14:26 reads, "In the fear of the LORD one has strong confidence, / and his children will have a refuge."

"The fear of the LORD" is a phrase found often in the books of the Old Testament. It's a very important concept that leads to a whole range of positive benefits, at least according to the writers of Proverbs. In sum, the phrase "fear of the LORD" means living life in the immediate presence of the mysterious and intrusive God of creation. There is no escaping this God, just as there is no controlling or limiting him. When we recognize that all of life—even what takes place behind surgery doors—is in the immediate presence of God, the result can be confidence for us and, for those we love, a refuge more secure than anything we might provide. The thing is, this God is not made in our image, susceptible to whims or commands. He is no shadow god.

The shadow of my created god is slowly giving way to something more substantial and real. It has been a long process, with a few "resonating moments" along the way. But slowly and steadily a mist has been lifting, and there to my absolute joy stands the God who made me. My created god has proven to be a shadow—appropriate, perhaps, for a time, but now fading. And with utter amazement I am beginning to realize that my search for God has turned into a pursuit by God. He, himself, broke my old images of the Divine and has replaced them with conceptions more substantive and true. With great and overwhelming delight I now realize that we are not here, primarily, to love God; but rather we are here to be loved by God! With this echo of God in mind, we can now turn our attention to those very real questions with which we began this chapter.

6

A GOOD GOD?

IN THE LAST CHAPTER, I concluded by suggesting that we are the objects of God's love. In the Bible, the Book of Job makes the point that, despite all evidence to the contrary, the very fact of our existence indicates that God desires and finds pleasure in the "work of [his] hands" (14:15). And there's the rub: How can the love of God be reconciled with something like a devastating illness, separation, and death? For doubters, settling questions about the reality of heaven begins with reconciling the goodness of God to the experience of tragedy. Minimizing the nature or fact of the tragedy in order to protect God's reputation simply will not do.

The reality of suffering and grief is only too apparent to anyone with eyes to see. The universe itself is largely an empty void interrupted by the violent crash and explosion of galaxies bumping into each other. And as far as we know, within this entire vast expanse, only here on earth does life exist; and that life is accompanied by pain, concluding in death. We cause pain when we begin life, and pain is our companion when we end our brief time. What kind of God would create a universe so filled with suffering, pain, and death?

As I struggled with the reality of my wife, Cher's, cancer, I gradually became aware that this, a deep disappointment in God, is the root of my struggle. I became angry with God.

Obviously, I must have retained a fundamental belief that God exists, for how can I be angry with someone who does not exist? So, given the reality of God's existence, it must be God's *goodness* that was in doubt. How could a good God create a universe with so much pain? At times it became overwhelming. I saw the devastation of my wife's illness repeated over and over in other families as we traveled from one hospital to another. Particularly troubling were those times when, sitting in a waiting room, we would be seated next to a person who had just received a diagnosis, and all the anxiety and questions with which they were being weighted down was easily read in their eyes. Then there were those persons who had no family from which to draw support. They would inevitably be sitting off in a corner, busily trying to occupy themselves with a magazine, and, failing to do so, eventually would sit staring at the floor, eyes red and expressionless.

Over those months, I found that I became much more sensitized to this sort of thing. Television news reports became harder to watch. The mounting death toll from the war in Iraq; descriptions of children dying alone and afraid in Sudan; and finally December 26, 2004, when nearly 200,000 people were suddenly and without warning swallowed up by the rising Indian Ocean in a massive tsunami. All these took on new urgency as I cursed God for creating a world so full of pain, suffering, and death. My image of the goodness of God crumbled and was replaced by a growing conviction that God was not to be trusted. I trust that I am not overly belaboring the point, but you must realize the depth, sincerity, and rage of this doubt. Doubters take things seriously, and the mixed evidence of God's goodness seems a more-than-sufficient reason to doubt heaven.

This deep disappointment that had been building haunted me for the better part of a year. I refused to ignore it, and I refused to be pacified. Much to my distress, the religious advice I received during this time was right along those lines.

"Just believe," I was told time and time again, as if belief were something that I could conjure up at will. And who would want that sort of faith? I had no desire to go through life playing pretend like some child with a stick in hand, conquering all the dragons infesting the backyard. No, like the writer of the opening lines of Psalm 73, a tremendous dissonance had developed between what I experienced and what I believed. Abandoning either end—my belief or the reality of what I was seeing around me—could easily eliminate the tension. Yet though the tension could be eliminated, it could not be resolved. And it could not answer Cher's question, "Do I have a future?"

When the resolution of this doubt finally did come, it was accompanied by joy—a joy more powerful than the rage that companioned the doubt. It wasn't simply a new idea or a new way of thinking that resolved the doubt. Rather, the discordant notes of doubt harmonized into a deep resonance of joy. Like Jacob wrestling with God all night and finding rest only at dawn (see Genesis 32), so too my rest came at dawn. I was driving alone at 5:00 A.M. on a deserted country road when an overwhelming sense of joy took hold of me. I began to sob and was forced to pull the car to the side of the road. My tears were not from grief or from anger, but out of complete joy.

Here is the reason and nature of my joy. My anger at God served as a constant reminder of the fact of his existence, and so that's where I started. This God who exists has done something, the evidence of which is all around us: He created. If God is good and intended to create a good and perfect creation, would not love be part of that created order? How could a created universe be perfect without love evident in it? And isn't this the real problem? Isn't love's absence the reason why the universe appears twisted and wrong? In my experience, at least, it is the enjoyment of love that makes the most pleasant and beautiful of all times. These include the memories of a picnic, or a walk in the woods, or a quiet sit on the swing shared by my wife or children. I confess, when I am immersed in love for those around me, I am at peace and fulfilled. When so engulfed by love, I have a sense of rightness within myself, as well as a sense of rightness about my experience of everything around me.

But that's the thing: Love is enjoyed best—if not only—when it is freely given. It cannot be forced or required or tricked; for when this happens, love becomes a hollow perversion of itself, cold and heartless. So, if a God who is good created this universe around us, he must have created it to be filled with the experience of love, at least for those who choose it. Since love is perfected only when it is freely given and freely received, it carries with it great risk.

Love's perfection demands the possibility of its refusal. And this seems to be exactly what has happened. God, in his love for us all, created a universe in which we too can experience love. In so doing, God took a great and cosmic risk. For in creating a universe in which we can share in love's possibility, he also created us to have choice either to freely accept that love or to reject it.

And love has been rejected with tragic consequences. Not only is the universe now peopled with agents able and quite willing to act from hatred and cruelty, the universe itself is filled with the manifold secondary and tertiary ripples of love's rejection. Like a child growing up in a home filled with hate and selfishness, she not only experiences the direct consequences of love's rejection (when cruelly hit or never hugged), she also experiences an environment devoid of love as the grocery money is spent at the bar and never on a present or warm clothes. The immediate act of love's rejection creates an environment devoid of the goodness, peace, and fulfillment that love produces.

We live in just such a home, you and I—a home in which love has been rejected. All of us have maltreated others and have been so treated by others. And the effects of our rejection of love have spread throughout the world of human experience. This is our doing, not the fault of God who made love's experience possible. More, our home has been invaded by others, spirit beings, evil and twisted and only too anxious to have us share their hatred and grief.

Suffering exists not because God has abandoned us or because he is a demon himself. Death, suffering, and pain are the results of a great gift that God has given to his creatures—a gift used poorly and in need of redemption. Love's loss is pain. As misers have always known, the easiest way to avoid pain is to avoid love. Yet, there is no joy on that road. And it was a joy so unexpected and overwhelming that convinced me there is another way.

On the side of the road at 5:00 A.M. that morning in late fall, a tremendous joy took hold of me as I realized the presence of love's potential. In no way, shape, or form am I saying that my wife's cancer, or any other bad thing that might afflict us, is the result of a personal sin, a deficient moral life, or the rejection of love. There is no use in pointing fingers. We are all in this together. There is no escape. We are all touched by pain. The point I'm trying to make is that these bad things, and the grief and pain they bring, are not evidence of God's abandonment of us or indicative of a demonic nature. The very fact of the pain, heartache, and terrible grief that death and suffering bring is evidence that disease, tragedy, and death are not the way things ought to be; we weren't created to find fulfillment with them. These things do bother us because they are contrary to the way we were made. Something went wrong, and love was rejected. The question is, can it be fixed? Can love be made the norm? In other words, can we hope in heaven? Or, as my wife, Cher, put it, "Do I have a future?" That's the road before us now.

PART 2:

A FORMING RESOLUTION

7

A VISION OF HOPE
IN THE WISDOM LITERATURE

Hope

If CHER, OR ANY OF us, has a future, that future will
express itself in the present by hope. What we *hope* figures
prominently in what possibilities we believe are held in our
future. Martin Heidegger, a prominent philosopher of the
twentieth century, believed that our view of the future in fact
forms a great deal of how we live life in the present (*Being
and Time*, translated by John Macquarrie and Edward
Robinson; Harper and Row, 1962). Young people go to
school because they want a good job. We put money aside in
IRAs because we expect to use it in days to come. Most of us
go to work for a whole week or two before we receive a pay-
check. Our futures help shape our present. The question
before us now is the shape of that future, and the way it
works out in a present hope.

Over the next several chapters, we are going to spend a
considerable amount of time examining some rather remarkable passages from the Bible. I present them to you not simply because they are found in the Bible. For doubters, the fact
that they are in the Bible does not lead to the conclusion that
they are therefore true. Rather, it is because these ideas and
concepts resonated deeply with the people who wrote the
passages that the ideas made their way into the Bible. And we
must apply the same test. In my quest, the ideas contained in

the next several chapters have become important signposts along the way, helping me to know which fork in the road to take. Perhaps they will do the same for you.

The words that are translated as "hope" in the Old Testament appear more frequently in Proverbs and Job than almost anywhere else. This is not an accident. Proverbs and Job are part of a subsection within the Old Testament called the Wisdom Literature. This special collection of literature (which includes Job, Proverbs, Ecclesiastes, and several of the Psalms) concerns itself with an open look at life. In this literature, the authors take a hard look at the world around us and at our place in this great, vast universe. The writers of the Wisdom Literature make observations, form theories, and draw conclusions about how best to get on in the world. That is, the Wisdom books give advice on how to live skillfully, advice on to how to function well. As we will see, hope is a big part of functioning well. Hopelessness can be quite dysfunctional, contrary to the way in which we were created. And misplaced hope or hope frustrated is worse than never having hope at all. This certainly seems to be what the writer of Proverbs had in mind: "Hope deferred makes the heart sick, / but a desire fulfilled is a tree of life" (13:12).

Consequently, it isn't enough to simply be hopeful. The authors of the Wisdom Literature are just as concerned over the appropriateness and reality of the object of the hope as they are with the expression of hope. Therefore, the often-repeated injunction to fear the LORD, and the also numerous statements of benefit coming from the fear of the LORD, show that hope is a topic frequently visited by the writers of the Wisdom books. As conceived by the writers of the Wisdom Literature, hope is an acknowledgement of the openness of the future (see for instance, Proverbs 10:28; 20:22; 23:17; 24:13-14). Hope is how the Wisdom writers answer my wife's question, "Do I have a future?"

Proverbs

Hope's foundation begins very simply. The writers of Proverbs envision the universe as an orderly whole, and because of that order, hope can be expressed. For example, the education of a son or a daughter can be filled with hope for discipline duly administered (19:18) and in good time will have its rewards in the character of the youth. In similar manner, both the righteous and the wicked are addressed in Proverbs. The righteous can, with good reason, have hope; but the wicked do so insincerely and therefore without joy (10:28). Behind this assessment lies the firm conviction that hope does have its rewards and that God will keep the hope of the righteous as a cherished reward: "The desire of the righteous ends only in good; / the expectation of the wicked in wrath" (11:23). According to this way of thinking, the decisions people make—leading to either a righteous or an unrighteous lifestyle—give hope its quality of authenticity: "Let not your heart envy sinners, / but continue in the fear of the LORD all the day. / Surely there is a future, / and your hope will not be cut off" (23:17-18).

All of this is to say two things. First, the writers of Proverbs believed the universe to be an act of creation invested with order and purpose, encouraging us to go and observe the functioning of the world around us in order to gain true wisdom (Proverbs 30). Whatever the processes that may have been and still are being used by the Creator, this much can be said: Functionality is a good clue to the true nature and reality of the world around us. The universal fact of human hope means that there is a reality that calls for our hope. There is a future. Second, the writers of Proverbs believed that hope can be either true or false. Hope itself is not enough. The object of hope is important, and, at this point, the writers of Proverbs are nudging us toward considering God himself as the object of our hope—that is, toward the fear of the LORD (*Reverberations of Faith: A Theological Handbook of Old Testament Themes*, by Walter

Brueggemann; Westminster John Knox, 2002; pages 100–01).

The admonition in Proverbs 23:17, to fear the LORD and not admire or be envious of bad people, is repeated in Proverbs 24:19-21. Fear of the LORD—or in other words, hope in God—is part of a moral lifestyle. A similar idea is presented in Psalm 37. There, words like "delight" (verse 4), "commit" and "trust" (verse 5), and "be still" and "wait" (verse 7) are used to describe this attitude of hope in God. And in both places, Psalm 37 and Proverbs 23–24, a future is offered to those who hope in God. A future and a hope that is not cut off is promised in both Proverbs 23:18 and 24:13-14. These assurances of a future lie nestled in a firm belief of a fixed order in the world—a world in which a future is the reward of the righteous, and a hope denied to the wicked and the fool (26:12; 29:20). This idea is stated very plainly in Proverbs 24, "Know that wisdom is [sweet like honey] to your soul; / if you find it, there will be a future, / and your hope will not be cut off" (verse 14, adapted).

The guarantor of this order is none other than God alone. Ultimately, it is not the future or things promised in the future upon which hope rests. Instead, hope rests in God himself (14:26; 22:19). "In the fear of the LORD one has strong confidence [hope], / and his children will have a refuge" (14:26, adapted).

Job

The Book of Job builds upon and to some extent challenges the conclusions that are offered in the Book of Proverbs. The storyline found in the Book of Job was popular throughout the ancient Near East. In this book, the main character, Job, is presented as a wealthy, prosperous, and righteous man. He attracts the attention of Satan, an accuser (quite distinct from the devil in later Christian tradition), who is granted an audience before God. Satan questions the integrity of Job and God by claiming that it is only because of Job's prosperity that he has hope in God. Satan is granted permission to test Job and subsequently Job is faced with horrendous loss. Nearly everything that is of any importance to Job is taken away—his health, his wealth, the lives of his children, and perhaps even his confidence in God is shaken. Everything that gave his life order and stability is violently torn from him. Job is taken back to the very basics of life. All the supports are knocked away. Able to rely upon nothing around him, Job asks: Can I have hope? That question becomes an entrance into one of the chief themes in the book—the effort to answer the question, *Who may hope?* In exploring the question, the writer of the book introduces us to several of Job's friends, each seeking to provide comfort and assistance in understanding his current plight. The speeches presented by Job's friends, and later answered by God, consider the possibility of hope for Job and for any of us. The discussion on the nature and extent of hope is developed through the dialogues in which Job's friends give voice to accepted ideas that are, in turn, challenged by Job. The dialogue starts with one of Job's friends, Eliphaz.

Eliphaz's Speech

Eliphaz begins the argument by reminding Job of how Job once had comforted others in their suffering and affliction. In so doing, Eliphaz gives voice to the standard religiously-accepted position of the day that states that the righteous may hope in God because of their righteousness (Job 4:3-9), "Think now, who that was innocent ever perished? / Or where were the upright cut off?" (4:7).

God himself becomes the basis of hope for the weak and righteous (5:8-16), while at the same time opposing the wicked and withholding hope from them. For "he saves the fatherless from [the] mouth [of the wicked], / the needy from the hand of the mighty. / So the poor have hope, / and injustice shuts her mouth" (5:15-16, adapted). Eliphaz's position is that the righteous, even if they are powerless, poor, and without social benefits, may have hope because of their righteousness. This is essentially the same position as articulated in the Book of Proverbs. Job is advised by Eliphaz to commit his troubles to God, for God does not leave the devout and weak without help. Unfortunately, the inverse of this belief was also held to be true: A devastation or an illness was viewed as evidence of some great moral failure. Eliphaz hints to Job that there must be some great sin behind Job's suffering, for surely only the wicked are devoid of hope (4:7-8).

Job does not agree with Eliphaz's assessment and instead rejects the help of this first friend (6:24-25). Job finds himself in the midst of a predicament in which comfort has fled from him and his previous confidence in God does not provide the help it once did. Job's experience does not affirm his belief. He is unwilling to deny the authenticity of his own experience, and since his faith will no longer assist him in understanding his predicament, doubt results (6:4, 8-10, 30).

It is important to remember that Job has thrown aside neither his experience nor his faith. He will not deny the reality of the tragedies that surround him, and still he values his relationship with God (7:11-21). The problem is that now the two are in discord. Doubt is the process of finding resolution. And it is this doubt that now threatens to engulf Job. Things will get worse before they get better.

Bildad's Speech

Job's second friend, Bildad, picks up the line of reasoning where the first friend, Eliphaz, left off (8:3-6). Bildad suggests that the very order upon which the universe was built implies a predictable, cause-and-effect relationship. Hope is inevitably present wherever there is righteousness, and, conversely, the wicked have no basis for hope:

> Can papyrus grow where there is no marsh?
> Can reeds flourish where there is no water?

> While yet in flower and not cut down,
>   they wither before any other plant.
> Such are the paths of all who forget God;
>   the hope of the godless man shall perish. (8:11-13)

This line of reasoning is based upon the notion of a divine order to the universe—that there are always answers to the question, *Why?* This created order extends to the moral sphere, where good behavior is rewarded and wicked people are punished. Accordingly, Bildad argues quite understandably that a lack of hope is evidence enough for a guilty verdict, as despair itself must indicate a lack of righteousness.

Zophar's Speech

Like a quick one-two punch, Bildad is followed by Job's third friend. What Bildad hinted at, Zophar expresses plainly: Job must have committed iniquity—sin—in order to find himself in his present condition (11:14-20). Hope is available to Job, according to Zophar; Job must only be righteous, and then he will have every reason to hope:

> If you set your heart aright,...
> You will forget your misery;
>   you will remember it as waters that have passed away....
> And you will have confidence, because there is hope;
>   you will be protected and take your rest in safety....
> But the eyes of the wicked will fail;
>   all way of escape will be lost to them,
>   and their hope is to breathe their last.
>   (11:13a, 16, 18, 20)

Job's Reply

Job's response to this all-too-common assignment of guilt is painfully clear. It is the expression of one who simply can't take any more, "In truth I have no help in me, / and any resource is driven from me" (6:13). Job's despair is so great that the only hope he has is death—that is, that there is no future—for all other hope has been stripped away (6:8-9). In despair he complains that a tree has more reason to hope than a man (14:1-2, 7). And here is the unnerving part: As Job sees it, this is God's fault. Job's complaint isn't that God has been indifferent or neglectful, but rather that God has been all too active:

> You destroy the hope of mortals.
> You prevail forever against them, and they pass away;
>   you change their countenance, and send them away....
> They feel only the pain of their own bodies,
>   and mourn only for themselves....
> [God] breaks me down on every side, and I am gone,
>   he has uprooted my hope like a tree.
>   (14:19b-20, 22; 19:10, NRSV)

The certain fate of death is preceded by pain and weakness. And to compound the physical deterioration, loneliness and isolation mount so that in the end, even mourners cannot be found. Perhaps the most devastating part of this whole loss of hope is the role played by God. Job comes very close to the conclusion that we earlier were forced to entertain: Perhaps God isn't a kind and good sovereign. Perhaps, there is a dark side of God. This disappointment with God ultimately leads to a challenge: "I cry to thee [God] and thou dost not answer me; I stand, and thou dost not heed me.... But when I looked for good, evil came; / and when I waited [hoped] for light, darkness came" (30:20, 26).

Job's dilemma isn't that he disagrees with his friends. Rather, Job finds himself in total agreement with them; hope *does* come from God. The trouble is that the once-taken-for-granted connection between hope and righteousness no longer looks assured. The cause-and-effect predictability that Job once believed governed the created universe no longer seems to apply, and it can't be trusted. By all standards, Job has lived a moral life, one in obedience to God. Yet now he finds himself in a situation in which all hope has been removed. Notice, it isn't the case that Job refuses to believe or obstinately has turned his back on God; rather, God has turned his back on Job and has taken hope with him. Job can't conjure up hope, nor can he produce hope by wishing it or piously living it.

Doubters understand this. When standing next to my wife's hospital bed, I had no more ability to generate hope then I did of flying to the moon. I was in need of a source of hope beyond my own doing. How surprising, then, is the end of Job's book. Even when forced to place his hand over his mouth, the dumbstruck Job learns that God agrees: Job has been more right than his friends:

> After the LORD had spoken these words to Job, the LORD said to Eliphaz the Temanite: "My wrath is kindled against you and against your two friends [Bildad and Zophar]; for you have not spoken of me what is right, as my servant Job has." (42:7)

What can this mean? It can be no other than simply this: God will not be tied down to a system in which he is manipulated by human conduct. The whole point of chapters 38–39 is to demonstrate that God acts freely without constraint, and in this, Job spoke rightly. Therefore, although devastating illness and disease or the tragedy and heartache so evident on the television news, is a present experience, it need not signal the absence of God or the loss of hope. How then does hope result? In pursuing the answer to this question, we move now to the Book of Ecclesiastes.

Ecclesiastes

The Book of Ecclesiastes is entitled *Qoheleth* in Hebrew (also spelled *Qohelet*) and is a wonderful book that has often gotten a bad rap. This Hebrew title, *Qoheleth*, is a descriptive term roughly equivalent in English to a great "speaker" or "preacher" ("The Book of Ecclesiastes," by W. Sibley Towner, in *The New Interpreter's Bible*, Vol. 5; Abingdon, 1997; pages 268–69). In today's terms, we might think of a newscaster, someone who gives the news of the day and tells it like it is. And that is exactly the goal of the Book of Ecclesiastes. The book is designed to give us insight into the nature of life. In fact, the central theme of Ecclesiastes is to answer the question, *Is there meaning to life?* Hope is mentioned only one place in the Book of Ecclesiastes (9:1-6). In this passage, the writer of Ecclesiastes makes the point that all humanity has the same fate—death. Death is the great equalizer. None of us will escape death, and there is no use in pretending that we will. That being the case, there is nothing better to do than to live the present moment, because "no one knows what is to happen, / and who can tell anyone what the future holds?" (10:14b, NRSV). So, "Just as you do not know how the breath comes to the bones in the mother's womb, so you do not know the work of God, who makes everything (11:5, NRSV).

In other words, the future belongs only to God. And this ownership is undisputed. Despite what we may or may not do, we are encouraged to "know that for all these things God will bring you into judgment" (11:9b, NRSV). So, come what may, one thing is certain: God holds the future. This means that questions about the future (such as Cher's question, "Do I have a future?") are really questions about God. This, then, brings us back full circle to Job.

The Creator Is the Basis for Hope

God's undisputed ownership of the future is foundational to Ecclesiastes (see 3:10-22). And this brings us back to Job, for Job shares this same conviction. While in Ecclesiastes this unshakable belief works itself out in a way of living today— advice to take hold of all the good in the present—in Job this belief concerning God's ownership of the future provides the basis for hope. And here is the amazing point made in Job. While experiencing a series of devastating events that bring death into the immediate, Job desperately longs to have hope for the future. He also knows that the future, whatever it may hold, belongs only to God. Herein lies the glimmer of hope. If God desires to have dealings with humanity in general and with each of us in particular, then there must be hope even for someone like Job, who is in the midst of a terrible despair. Can death limit a future held by God? Or can the Creator intend death for what he has created?

This theme of hope in God is developed over several chapters in the heart of the Book of Job. The beginning point is filled with anguish concerning the present. But even in that anguish, Job envisions that there must be more: "O that you [God] would hide me in Sheol [the grave], / that you would conceal me until your wrath is past, / that you would appoint me a set time, and remember me!" (Job 14:13, NRSV).

In the statement from Job 14:13—a cry, really—Job is willing to admit that his present devastation and the imminent threat of death is, somehow or other, God's doing. Job is willing to concede that point to his friends. But there's more. The last line of the verse allows in a glimmer of hope. *Sheol*, the grave, cannot erase God's memory. Job's hope isn't simply that God would memorialize him, but rather that God would bring restoration. There is a "time" appointed for him beyond the grave; there is a future.

Later in the same chapter, Job explains the basis for his future hope beyond the grave. Even if his present experience of devastation is a sign of God's displeasure (a point that Job will allow only for the sake of argumentation; he never does, in fact, agree to this idea and later is vindicated by God for his refusal to do so), Job is convinced that the same desire that led God to create will lead God to redeem:

> If mortals die, will they live again?
> All the days of my service I would wait
> until my release should come.
> You [God] would call, and I would answer you;
> you would long for the work of your hands.
> (Job 14:14-15, NRSV)

God will long for *the work of his hands*; that's *Job!* There is a future waiting, an all-embracing future based upon the fact of creation itself. For Job, the very fact that he exists, that God chose to create him, is proof enough that there is a future beyond the grave. It isn't just Job's future that is at stake, but God's too. If the grave dismantles what God created, then God, too, is the loser, for the grave would rob God of the pleasure that motivated his act of creation. And since it is beyond comprehension that God would be the perpetrator of some moral ill and therefore suffer the loss of his own future, Job has confidence that his misfortune is not evidence of guilt either. Job's future is intertwined inseparably with God's future.

To be sure, we get only a glimmer of this deep hope in chapter 14, for the overwhelming despair that Job feels is not conquered yet, and it quickly reasserts itself. The all-too-evident fact of Job's devastating illness, the death of his family, and the loss of his possessions still calls for some resolution. A "making it right" or redemption of sorts is needed. That redemptive cry begins to find voice in chapter 16:

> O earth, cover not my blood,
>   and let my cry find no resting place.
> Even now, behold, my witness is in heaven,
>   and he that vouches for me is on high.
> My friends scorn me;
>   my eye pours out tears to God,
> that he would maintain the right of a man with God,
>   like that of a man with his neighbor. (16:18-21)

As Walther Zimmerli points out in his book, *Man and His Hope in the Old Testament*, these verses are part of a legal presentation (SCM Press, 1971; page 23). Although hope is not expressly mentioned here, hope is in the background of this argument that asserts the rights of a mortal with God. Job claims that just as a person can justly maintain certain rights with his neighbor, a person also can legitimately assert rights before God. What are those rights? Only this: That God has once said yes to Job's right to life; and that the argument of Job's friends, which denies his right to life before God, is a deception and a lie. Job pleads that his blood not be covered up, that his cry of murder not be squelched (verse 18). Job will have his day in court, and God himself will be called upon as witness to testify that indeed, Job does have the right to life. The Creator will affirm the creature's right to life.

The courtroom imagery is carried into chapter 19. This time, God as witness is replaced by the image of God as judicial figure: "For I know that my Redeemer lives, / and that at the last he will stand upon the earth; / and after my skin has been thus destroyed, / then [without] my flesh I shall see God" (19:25-26, NRSV, adapted; Zimmerli; pages 23–24).

In this dispute, the speaker is considering his own death as a completed fact. For the sake of the argument being presented, he has already died. It's as if the blood is already shed, the skin is already destroyed. Herein lies the strength of the words. Even in death, Job knows that he has hope—that there is someone who will stand up for him and see to it that his right as creation will be restored. Job's right to life is guaranteed, not because of anything that he has done but because the Creator has chosen to create.

And this is important. Job's friends were attempting to argue the right to hope based upon a person's moral character—that is, God is bound to act beneficially in the future based upon the integrity of the person today. But Job will have nothing to do with this argument. Instead, he argues that hope is assured, not because of anything he has done, but simply on the basis that God has created and that God will not abandon his creation. It is in God alone, and in his past and evident acts of creation, that hope is assured.

The concluding speeches by God in the Book of Job drive this point home. Repeatedly, chapters 38–41 assert the sufficiency of God as Creator. Creation itself is called to witness to Job; and in the face of this undisputable evidence, Job's protests must vanish away. Job has spoken rightly (see 42:7), but he has not understood the full import of his own words—and this, now, God explains to him. Job has a right to life (a future) given to him by the Creator. And the Creator himself will defend that right.

When you stop and let the full impact of these ideas from Job sink in, it can be overwhelming. God has said yes to each of us. There is a future. Just as surely as there is a Creator, there is a future for all that God has chosen to create. Whenever hope is based upon human effort, ingenuity, or piety, it is destined to fail, as it did in Job. However, the fact of creation provides a firm and unassailable basis for hope based solely upon the Creator. God does take pleasure in "the work of his hands." Death still hurts. At times the grief can be overwhelming, and it lasts a long time. But it is not the end. Somehow or other, the Creator has provided a future—a heaven. In the next chapter, we will see just how fully that hope is dominated by God himself.

8

A VISION OF HOPE
IN THE PSALMS

IN THE LAST CHAPTER, WE learned that hope for the future is intimately connected to hope in God. The future is more about a person than it is a place or a thing. Consequently, doubts about heaven are, in the final analysis, doubts about God. And from God's standpoint this is no light concern; because, as we discovered, God has committed the quality of his "future" to the quality of ours. The Creator remembers and takes pleasure in us, his creation, to the extent that if our future were cut short by death, his future would be affected too.

We are now going to broaden our search by considering what the Psalms may have to say about our quest for heaven. The Psalms were the prayer book for the worship of the Old Testament community of faith. As such, the Psalms can give us insight into how that group of people thought about their questions concerning the future. If they saw a connection between their expectations concerning heaven and the trust-worthiness of God, it ought to be given expression in the Psalms. If they had confidence in God's ownership of the future, we ought to expect that the Psalms will be richly filled with visions of hope. The reader of the Psalms, with this expectation, is not disappointed. Questions about the future and about life in a difficult present are never far away when God is addressed in this collection of songs and prayers.

Before we begin our search, two things must first be said about visions of hope in the Psalms. The first has to do with vocabulary. The Psalms are rich in their use of words to create images and expressions that capture the full gamut of human emotion and experience. In the Psalms, the idea of hope is conveyed by a wide range of terms (calling on, waiting on, confidence in, trust), more so than what we find in the Proverbs or Job. And there is a reason for this. In the Psalms, hope is characteristic of an interpersonal relationship. God himself is the object of hope and hope characterizes those who fix their eyes on him. When pursuing a vision of hope in the Psalms, we will allow ourselves to broaden our search to include these various terms as well.

The second thing that must be said about looking for visions of hope in the Psalms has to do with the structure of the collection. The Hebrew name for the collection of Psalms translates into something like "songs of praise." The title makes use of the same Hebrew word that is elsewhere used to elicit praise to God (*hallelujah*) and emphasizes that the whole group of Psalms is about giving praise to God (*The Psalms: An Introduction*, by James L. Crenshaw; Eerdmans, 2001). For the modern reader, the idea that the whole collection of Psalms is about giving praise to God takes some getting used to; for only a small portion of the Psalms resemble the inspirational choruses and songs that are currently popular among worshiping groups. The Psalms collection is not one but actually five different books (Book 1: Psalms 1–41; Book 2: Psalms 42–72; Book 3: Psalms 73–89; Book 4: Psalms 90–106; Book 5: Psalms 107–50), composed of a variety of different types of songs (praise songs, petition songs, laments, wisdom songs, royal songs, and so forth). As we read the Psalms, it is important for us to remember that we are reading a wide variety of different types of songs, and that each different type addresses human experiences and conditions from a slightly different vantage point and so offers slightly different nuances to a vision of hope.

Psalm 1: Prologue

We'll begin our examination of the Psalms at the beginning. Psalm 1 is intended to function as a prologue to the entire collection and so sets the stage for the rest to follow. As such, the psalm urges the reader to follow a path of righteousness in the here and now. At times, this psalm wasn't considered part of the collection itself but may have functioned as a preface of sorts. This is made evident in that some versions of Acts 13:33 label the quotation made there as coming from "Psalm 1," when it is actually from Psalm 2, as noted in our modern collection of Psalms.

Psalm 1 describes two types of people, the righteous and the unrighteous. Although the word is never used in this psalm, *hope* is a quality offered to the righteous but withheld from the unrighteous. For the person who meditates on "the law of the LORD" is like a healthy and productive tree that enjoys a reliable and constant water supply. The wicked, however, enjoy no such stability but are like chaff, wind-blown, shriveled, and quickly disappearing. A future is promised to the righteous, but only destruction is promised to the wicked (verses 3-6).

In presenting hope as an expected consequence of a moral life, Psalm 1 sounds very much like the position articulated by Job's friends. But we read this psalm correctly when we recognize that its main point isn't some sort of cause-and-effect relationship in which hope can be predicted. The main point of the psalm is that the future belongs only to God, and hope for the future comes only from his hand: "For the LORD knows the way of the righteous, / but the way of the wicked will perish" (1:6).

Because the future belongs to God, and since the godless have chosen a different path, they are, therefore, confronted by a much different future, one quite hopeless, whether they know it or not. This psalm can escape the negative verdict given to Job's friends only by recognizing that it is designed to urge the listener to godliness in the here and now—and that in so doing, it holds out the promise of a hope freely given to those who hold to God and his word. The psalm is intended to encourage the reader to meditate on "the law of the LORD."

Psalm 37 is similar in its intent to that of Psalm 1. The following two verses in chapter 37 press home the point.

> For the wicked shall be cut off;
>   but those who wait for [hope in] the LORD shall possess
>   the land. . . .
> Wait for [hope in] the LORD, and keep to his way,
>   and he will exalt you to possess the land. (37:9, 34a)

These verses present two admonitions to "wait" upon the LORD. Hope, presented here as waiting, is an attitude of complete openness to the LORD , recognizing that the future is solely in his care. This openness to God is exactly what the writers of the Wisdom Literature are talking about when they admonish the reader to "fear the LORD"—that is, to live life in the immediate presence of the mysterious and intrusive Creator God.

Psalm 1 prepares us to expect something from God. We are to expect a degree of enhanced functionality of the kind that we talked about in the first part of this book (see pages 33–35). The psalm uses a word picture of a tree planted beside a reliable and steady supply of water to describe the person who has learned to depend upon God's law. That person lives well, and can function, because of the nourishing supply given by God.

So, to summarize, Psalm 1 states in no uncertain terms that God holds the future. To maintain hope, we need to be open to the Creator God. That openness will help make us "functional," like a tree planted beside an unfailing supply of water. That constant water supply is a painted portrait of

God's law. We would do well to give attention, for a moment at least, to just what is meant by God's "law" or "word." And the place to do that, like no other in the entire collection of Psalms, is Psalm 119.

Psalm 119: Hope and the Word of God

By anybody's standard, Psalm 119 is a literary masterpiece. This psalm is an enormous acrostic, each group of eight verses beginning with the successive letter of the Hebrew alphabet. This is no simple feat, as anyone who has ever played the alphabet game can attest! Pride of place, the central focus in this psalm, is God's word—God's advice, precepts, and direction. God's "word," in this psalm and elsewhere in the Bible, is not referring to a Bible we would pick up today, but refers to God's active engagement and self-disclosure in history, however it may be communicated. Whatever the means—whether it be a written page, a vision, or an answer to prayer—the emphasis is not on the means of communication, but on the fact that this is *God* communicating.

Hope is a frequent companion of God's self-disclosure. As Psalm 119 describes, God's active engagement and self-disclosure become a focal point for the development of hope (see verses 49, 81, 114, 147). The word of God that gives guidance and help for the present is also able to provide security and comfort—hope for the future.

> Remember thy word to thy servant,
>   in which thou hast made me hope.
> This is my comfort in my affliction
>   that thy promise gives me life....
> Thou art my hiding place and my shield;
>   I hope in thy word....
> I rise before dawn and cry for help;
>   I hope in thy words. (Psalm 119:49-50, 114, 147)

But here's the thing. Hope is not a mechanistic result of simply reading words on a page, or even memorizing some favorite verses. It is *God's* active engagement being communicated, by means of the words, that brings the hope. And we must never forget this. The psalmist here is talking about that deep-seated resonance, or God-echo, that comes when we can feel the truth of what we are reading or hearing. And as many doubters can attest, with our psalmist this God-echo is often accompanied by distress that robs one of sleep or that is expressed with tears. The comfort comes when God is near: "But thou art near, O LORD, / and all thy commandments are true.... Plead my cause and redeem me; / give me life according to thy promise!" (119:151, 154).

God is near, not when he actually changes location, but when his presence is made evident through a tangible sense of comfort, security, and empathy. This takes a variety of forms, but once experienced it is never forgotten.

We shouldn't lose sight of the fact that the one who waits for God in this manner is a spring of joy for the whole community of believers: "Those who fear thee shall see me and rejoice, / because I have hoped in thy word" (119:74). The psalmist's stories of faith became an encouragement to those around him. Undoubtedly, those around the psalmist knew of his plight and the devastating crises that occasioned the hope. They shared his journey with him. Psalm 119 begins to introduce us to the communal or social vision of hope in the Old Testament. To be sure, hope is found only in God; yet there is a sense in which that hope is expressed through the lives of those who recognize their dependency upon the LORD.

A frequent byproduct of a devastating illness, tragedy, or death of a loved one is that it is accompanied by a sense of loneliness and isolation. For many of us, grief is a very difficult thing to share. It makes us uncomfortable, both as the one sharing the grief and as the friend accepting the shared burden. Yet Psalm 119 suggests that there is a dynamic of healing and hope that expresses itself when the burden is carried by more than one (verse 74). I don't pretend to know how it works, or why. But I have seen it happen. Maybe it's part of that God-echo still resident within us, telling us that we need each other. We function better when we are connected to other people in a meaningful fashion. This is true in shadow times just as much as in times of bright sunshine.

The Laments

Today, no less than when the Psalms were written, people who find themselves comfortable and without need talk less about hope than do those who find themselves in need and despair. When the need is greatest, hope is dearest. For those in need, there are a number of psalms that can be very helpful. These psalms, sometimes labeled "Laments," have much to offer the person in search of hope.

In my opinion, the Lament psalms are perhaps the most overlooked part of the entire Old Testament. They are hard to read, for the strength of emotion can be frightening. Fortunately, however, the Laments are being rediscovered (Crenshaw; pages 142–54). They are particularly helpful for doubters, for the questions raised in the Laments are also the questions that preoccupy people trying to make faith and experience fit together. In these psalms, the props have been kicked away, and once-assumed beliefs and ideas are now open for question. The opening of Psalm 69 is a good example: "Save me, O God! / For the waters have come up to my neck" (verse 1a).

For me, Psalm 69:2 will now and forever be associated with images of the tsunami that devastated coastlines throughout the Indian Ocean in December of 2004. The images that open this psalm—those of rising water, swirling with mire preventing any possibility of a foothold or climb to safety—must capture only a small fraction of the horror that must have overwhelmed so many people as the unstoppable tidal surge swept everything away. Similarly, the psalmist had no refuge, no place to hide, and no place to regain his footing. In his words, "I have come into deep waters, / and the flood sweeps over me" (verse 2b). Help is not to be found. Perhaps most discouraging of all, however, the psalmist senses failure and disappointment in store for those who search for God: "I am weary with my crying; / my throat is parched. / My eyes grow dim / with waiting for my God" (verse 3). Even family, brothers and sisters, are unwilling to offer assistance or comfort (see verse 8). And like the writer of Psalm 119, our psalmist here in Psalm 69 also recognizes the social element of hope: "Insults have broken my heart, / so that I am in despair. I looked for pity, but there was none; / and for comforters, but I found none" (verse 20).

"I found none." Those are difficult words, and they are perhaps fully understood only by those who have experienced the isolation that devastation brings. Now, when the psalmist is placed in a position to need the encouragement of others, none is to be found. This is not to say that he denies the fact that God alone is the source of hope, but only that he recognizes that those who, like him, have sought God were of no help. If we hearken back to Job's description, such people were "miserable comforters" (Job 16:2)—an apt label for hollow gestures of aid. And as Psalm 25 indicates, this can be a long and drawn-out experience. Psalm 25:5 says that the psalmist was waiting on God "all the day long." That description doesn't mean consistency in the sense of waiting all day without a break. Rather, the psalmist is giving vent to the apparent futility of the waiting: To that point, at any rate, God was a no-show.

The experience of hope shaken or vanishing altogether can have a variety of causes. In Psalm 38, the psalmist tells us that it was God himself who struck him down with illness, and that his sin has become all too evident to him, leading to a whole new form of mental distress:

> O LORD, rebuke me not in thy anger,
>   nor chasten me in thy wrath!

> For thy arrows have sunk into me,
> and thy hand has come down on me.
>
> There is no soundness in my flesh
> because of thy indignation;
> there is no health in my bones
> because of my sin.
> For my iniquities have gone over my head;
> they weigh like a burden too heavy for me.
>
> My wounds grow foul and fester
> because of my foolishness,
> I am utterly bowed down and prostrate;
> all the day I go about mourning.
> For my loins are filled with burning,
> and there is no soundness in my flesh.
> I am utterly spent and crushed;
> I groan because of the tumult of my heart. (38:1b-8)

As the psalmist expresses it, his initial crisis has only magnified, as now, heaped up are a sense of God's anger and the psalmist's own emotional despair. Yet despite the desperateness of the hour and the admitted self-deficiencies and sin, it is still only God on whom hope is cast:

> But for thee, O LORD, do I wait;
> it is thou, O LORD my God, who wilt answer....
> Do not forsake me, O LORD!
> O my God, be not far from me!
> Make haste to help me,
> O Lord, my salvation! (38:15, 21-22)

Hope's loss isn't always due to the sudden and unexpected devastation that sometimes crosses our paths. For many of us, hope's loss is simply because of the slow and relentless march of time. In Psalm 71 it is the debilities of age (see verse 18) contrasted with the memories of youth (see verse 5) that seem to give the psalmist pause to question the future: "Do not cast me off in the time of old age; / forsake me not when my strength is spent" (verse 9). Consider the conclusion of Psalm 27: "Wait for the LORD; / be strong, and let your heart take courage; / yea, wait for the LORD!" (verse 14).

This isn't a measure of good advice from some third party, but rather it is the conclusion to a self-conversation in which the options of divine disappointment have been weighed and found to lead to no other source of hope. "Thou hast said, 'Seek ye my face.' / My heart says to thee, / 'Thy face, LORD, do I seek.' / Hide not thy face from me" (27:8-9a).

Likewise, Psalm 130, with a deep awareness of the length and breadth of anguish, concludes that this psalm writer has hope: "I wait for the LORD, my soul waits, / and in his word I hope" (verse 5). And for others there is no substitute for hope placed in God: "O Israel, hope in the LORD! / For with the LORD there is steadfast love, / and with him is plenteous redemption" (verse 7).

Built upon these confidences, Psalms 42–43 express hope in the form of a restoration of past encounters with God:

> Why are you cast down, O my soul,
>   and why are you disquieted within me?
> Hope in God; for I shall again praise him,
>   my help and my God.
> My soul is cast down within me,
>   therefore I remember thee
> from the land of Jordan and of Hermon,
>   from Mount Mizar. (42:5-6)

> Why are you cast down, O my soul,
>   and why are you disquieted within me?
> Hope in God; for I shall again praise him,
>   my help and my God. (43:5)

Notice it isn't the elimination of uncomfortable and disappointing experiences that forms the content of the psalmist's hope; rather it is the life, once joyfully received from God, that becomes the guarantee that God will not leave him disappointed and without hope. Job's confidence was stated generally, but it was the same confidence. Job trusted that he had a future based upon the fact of his existence—that God took pleasure in the work of God's hands. The psalmist is saying the very same thing. He is saying it simply in terms of his own life experience. The psalmist brings to mind episodes when that divine pleasure in the work of his hands was very real and evident. Those memories provide the link to a hopeful future. God does not leave incomplete any project, work, or person that he has begun!

This same sentiment provides the basis for Paul's assurance for the Philippians: "And I am sure that he who began a good work in you will bring it to completion at the day of Jesus Christ" (Philippians 1:6).

That "good work" brought to completion is the redemption of all of life. And redemption is nothing less than the unfettered expression of divine joy over what he has made.

Psalms of Faith

If the Laments are at one end of the spectrum, way over on the other end is another set of psalms, often referred to as the "Praise Psalms" or "Psalms of Faith." These psalms too make frequent reference to God as the source of hope, but they do so from quite a different angle (Crenshaw; pages 34–37).

Psalm 62 has a repeating phrase that expresses a quiet confidence in God: "For God alone my soul waits in silence; / from him comes my salvation.... For God alone my soul waits in silence, / for my hope is from him" (62:1b, 5).

Psalm 131 presents a wonderful picture of the calming effects of hope in God: "But I have calmed and quieted my soul, / like a child quieted at its mother's breast; / like a child that is quieted is my soul. O Israel, hope in the LORD / from this time forth and for evermore" (131:2-3). In all the Psalms, there is perhaps no more tender or moving image of God's care and support; and having been "tucked in" once myself, I can tell you there is no more comforting experience.

Yet we must not lose sight of the corporate aspect of God's provision of hope. At the end of Psalm 31, hope in God strengthens the whole believing group: "Be strong, and let your heart take courage, / all you who wait for [hope in] the LORD!" (verse 24).

Psalm 146 expresses the conviction that help is available to those who hope in God: "Happy is he whose help is the God of Jacob, / whose hope is in the LORD his God, / who made heaven and earth, / the sea, and all that is in them; / who keeps faith for ever" (146:5-6). The plain evidence that this hope is not misplaced is the fact of creation all around. And the continuing rhythms of creation give credibility to the reliability or trustworthiness of God.

That *help* mentioned in Psalm 146 is described in other places as well. In Psalm 33, help is in the form of protection: "Our soul waits for the LORD; / he is our help and shield" (verse 20).

Psalm 147 adds a whole new dimension. As we have seen throughout the Psalms, hope is granted for the benefit of those of us who need hope desperately. But we aren't the only ones to benefit. In Psalm 147, the psalmist expresses that our hope is a great delight to God: "But the LORD takes pleasure in those who fear him, / in those who hope in his steadfast love" (verse 11).

In fact, all creation is invited to join the circle of joy created by hope in God:

> These all look to you
>> to give them their food in due season. (104:27, NRSV)

> The eyes of all look to you,
>> and you give them their food in due season.
> You open your hand,
>> satisfying the desire of every living thing.
>> (145:15-16, NRSV)

Pulling It Together

We have taken a whirlwind tour through the Psalms in search of hope. From all that we have surveyed, two ideas stand out. Both of these contributions from the Psalms are key signposts pointing, giving us direction, in our quest for heaven.

The first signpost is this: Hope is in God alone. In contrast to the polytheistic (belief in more than one god) worldviews of Israel's neighbors and of many Israelites themselves, the psalmists all were convinced that only one source of hope is possible (*The Religions of Ancient Israel: A Synthesis of Parallactic Approaches*, by Ziony Zevit; Continuum, 2001). In that respect, the psalmists were countercultural. They went against the grain, not apparently from some desire to be individualistic, but because the strength of their experience taught them that hope in God provided a help not to be found anywhere else. Hope cannot even be produced by human initiative. Hope cannot be self-manufactured, nor can it be sustained by reliance upon other temporary supports. Only God the Creator will do.

The second observation builds on the first, and it considers the certainty of a hope that is fixed upon God. We'll begin considering this certainty in Psalm 39. This may seem like a strange place to talk about the certainty of hope in God, for Psalm 39 is one of the most difficult psalms I know. It gives expression to the deepest of human distress and anxiety. The psalmist's mortality and prospect of nothingness loom large: "LORD, let me know my end, / and what is the measure of my days; / let me know how fleeting my life is. / You have made my days a few handbreadths, / and my lifetime is as nothing in your sight. / Surely everyone stands as a mere breath" (verses 4-5, NRSV).

Life is short—for all of us—and the prospect of nothingness is a dreaded and unwelcome guest. The thought produces a world without hope and certainly without a future:

Hear my prayer, O LORD,
  and give ear to my cry;
  hold not thy peace at my tears!
For I am thy passing guest,
  a sojourner, like all my fathers.
Look away from me, that I may know gladness,
  before I depart and be no more! (39:12-13)

In the midst of this terrible experience of hopelessness, there is an unmistakable doubt about God. A prayer is voiced in hopes of gaining God's attention, while at the same time the prayer is itself a request that God turn away and relent from his mistreatment of the psalmist. Yet right in the middle of this confusion, we have a quite unexpected statement of firm confidence: "And now, Lord, for what do I wait? / My hope is in thee" (39:7). The psalmist lays himself bare before God. In so doing, not even his deep, heartfelt anxiety about God is hidden. How can it be that in the middle of this deep doubt and confusion, hope revives? How does this statement of confidence coexist with doubt?

A song from Lamentations adds welcome insight. In Lamentations 3:18-25, we are confronted by the possibility of hope:

So I say, "Gone is my glory,
  and my expectation from the LORD."

Remember my affliction and my bitterness,
  the wormwood and the gall!
My soul continually thinks of it
  and is bowed down within me.
But this I call to mind,
  and therefore I have hope:

The steadfast love of the LORD never ceases,
  his mercies never come to an end;
they are new every morning;
  great is thy faithfulness.

"The LORD is my portion," says my soul,
"therefore I will hope in him."

The LORD is good to those who wait for him,
to the soul that seeks him.

The song begins with deep despair: Gone; all hope is gone. But by the time we get to verse 21, a surprising conclusion meets us: Even if the loss of hope is due to the perceived anger of God, there is hope that the anger is momentary, and that, always, "the LORD is my portion." The certainty of hope is grounded in the firm foundation that God himself *is my portion*. This description of God as "my portion" comes from far back in the Israelite collective memory. As described in the Book of Joshua (chapters 13 through 23), the Promised Land was divided among the conquering Israelite tribes, with each tribe receiving its portion. A piece of territory was allotted to each tribe; each tribe, that is, but one. One tribe was excluded, for the LORD was their inheritance (Joshua 13:33). In a very real sense, that tribe was cast upon God for their food, their shelter, and their future.

And now, we have received the same legacy. Psalm 73 is in full agreement. Utter despair is revived into hope when it is remembered that God, himself, is "my portion":

Nevertheless I am continually with thee;
   thou dost hold my right hand.
Thou dost guide me with thy counsel,
   and afterward thou wilt receive me to glory.
Whom have I in heaven but thee?
   And there is nothing upon earth that I desire besides
   thee.
My flesh and my heart may fail,
   but God is the strength of my heart and my portion for
   ever. (Psalm 73:23-26)

Because God is my portion, and because the future is firmly held in God's grasp, hope is renewed. "God is my portion": This statement contains all the hope and confidence of a certain future. Where God makes himself available as a person's "portion," neither death nor life, nor principalities nor powers, nor any other thing is able to hinder the one who is so held by God (Romans 8:38-39).

And this is perhaps the most valuable lesson so far on our journey. Doubt is not resolved by the addition of new information. In the quest for heaven, it isn't certitude that resolves doubt, but *trust*.

9

A VISION OF HOPE
IN THE TORAH

At THIS POINT, OUR JOURNEY has shown us that our quest for heaven is not so much a search for what or where, but a search for *who*. God is the object of our quest. Our future is in the hands of God, who has made himself available to us as our "portion"—that is, our hope. Hope is not a human invention. Instead, hope is a byproduct of, as the Wisdom writers would tell us, living life in the presence of God.

The problem with our search so far is that it has all been a bit abstract. We've read many statements and gained some knowledge about what some of the writers of the Old Testament thought and experienced. This knowledge can be useful, but it isn't until it resonates deeply within that the hope really begins to take shape. Hope comes from God, not from information *about* God. It is in meeting God that hope is born. If these statements are true and accurately reflect the vision of hope in the Old Testament, then we should rightly expect that hope is characteristic of the stories in the Bible that depict interactions between God and people. In this chapter, we are going to take a brief look at some of the opening narratives of the Bible to see if indeed God is a God of hope.

The Torah, made up of the first five books of the Bible, is, in many respects, the most important part of the Old Testament. A good argument can be made for saying that all of the rest of the Old Testament sprang from this core of five books (*Heavenly Torah: As Refracted Through the Generations*, by Abraham Joshua Heschel, edited and translated by Gordon Tucker; Continuum, 2006; page 61). But the Torah is not all of one cloth. In these books we have a complex of voices and experiences woven together into one whole. One of the striking things to first greet the reader of the Torah is the story-like quality of most of the material. In the pages of the first five books of the Bible, we aren't presented with an academic discussion on God or on our relation to God. Rather, we read stories that provide concrete examples of how God deals with people. In our search for a vision of hope in the Torah, we will survey a number of those stories.

Creation

A good place to begin our survey is with the story of Creation. As many have pointed out, the Creation narrative of Genesis is not one story, but several stories woven together to form its present structure ("Introduction," by E. A. Speiser, in *The Anchor Bible, Genesis*; Doubleday, 1964; pages xxiv–xxix). While chapter 1 of Genesis presents a majestic overview and cosmic perspective of Creation, it is beginning with Genesis 2:4 that we find the part of the story that zeroes in on the place of humanity and on God's relation to this special part of the work of his hands.

In Genesis 2:7, a man is created by God. Adam is given the breath of life and so becomes a living being. Dependent upon God right from the beginning, the man is placed in a garden and given an environment in which all hope (i.e., future life) is a present reality. Hope, experience, and functionality all meet together in perfect harmony. But it isn't long until a need arises. In Genesis 2:18, we read that God says, "It is not good that the man should be alone," and so God makes a companion for him. When a need is discovered, when a hope is unmet, God steps in to resolve the situation, and the result is, as the man said, "This at last [read: hope fulfilled] is bone of my bones" (2:23).

Within the scope of this whole perfect environment, only one limitation is given to the newly created man: "But of the tree of the knowledge of good and evil you shall not eat, for in the day that you eat of it you shall die" (2:17). In this one stipulation, the man is reminded of the Giver behind the gift of life. Far too often, attention has been directed toward trying to figure out the nature of the tree that is forbidden, and in so doing the clear connection between Giver and gift has been ignored. Should the command be violated, death results—the loss of future and hope. If, however, the man remains faithful to the Creator, then life remains full of future and hope. The main point of the verse is that God alone authors life. Future and hope are gifts given by his hand.

The command to not eat of the tree provides occasion for the plot to thicken. A new voice enters the story in chapter 3. The serpent, part of the created universe, suggests that eating the fruit would result in a Godlike ability to control the future: "The serpent said to the woman, 'You will not die. For God knows that when you eat of it your eyes will be opened, and you will be like God, knowing good and evil'" (3:4-5).

According to the serpent's advice, eating of the fruit would give to the man and woman power over everything. The phrase "knowing good and evil" should not be construed narrowly in a moralistic fashion, like "knowing right from wrong." Instead, the phrase represents a device often used in Hebrew literature in which opposites are paired to indicate totality (similar to the English phrases "day and night" or "heaven and earth" or "up from down").

Eve considered what the serpent had to say and concluded that, among other things, the tree "was to be desired to make one wise" (3:6). *Wisdom* is an extremely important word in this whole episode. It doesn't mean latent intelligence in the sense that eating fruit from the tree would make her smart. Instead, and as we have seen from its frequent use in the Wisdom Literature, the word *wise* or *wisdom* describes the ability to cope with life—the ability to handle things. A wonderful example of the benefits of wisdom and its corollaries is found in the opening of the Book of Proverbs (1:1-6), where a truly amazing list of character qualities is promised to the one who will take seriously the advice offered. *Wisdom* is a word that describes skill in living.

Later writers in the Wisdom Literature claim that wisdom is grounded upon "fear of the LORD." In Genesis 3, the serpent makes just the opposite claim, suggesting that a skillful life is found independent from God. The man and the woman both give in to this tempting voice, and so forfeit hope and future. The man is told: "In the sweat of your face you shall eat bread till you return to the ground, for out of it you were taken; you are dust, and to dust you shall return" (Genesis 3:19).

The comparison to statements made in Job and Ecclesiastes is unmistakable:

> Man that is born of a woman is of few days, and full of
> trouble.
> He comes forth like a flower, and withers;
> he flees like a shadow, and continues not. (Job 14:1-2)

> For the fate of the sons of men and the fate of beasts is the same; as one dies, so dies the other. They all have the same breath, and man has no advantage over the beasts; for all is vanity. (Ecclesiastes 3:19)

Although there are similarities between the statements in Genesis and those in Ecclesiastes and Job, there is one big difference. In Genesis, while grasping after a hope and future that he can control (taking matters into his own hands), the man finds himself without a future by separating himself from God, who alone is future-generating and future-governing. The man's attempt to manufacture and secure his own future by eating from the tree, in fact, separated him from his only source of hope and future: the Creator God. Yet, amazingly, the story does not end here. In all this, God still offers hope.

Perhaps because the story is so familiar to us it has lost some of its impact. Surrounded now by the threat of death and hopelessness, the man and woman are suddenly given the promise of hope. In Genesis 3:15-16, a new generation is promised to the man and woman, and with that new generation, a future and hope. Children will be born, and life will continue. This promise of a future is recognized and reflected in the name that Adam gives to Eve, "mother of all living" (3:20).

Cain and Abel

Immediately after the account of hope lost in Creation, reinforcement is provided by the story of brother murdering brother in Genesis 4.

Cain said to Abel his brother, "Let us go out to the field." And when they were in the field, Cain rose up against his brother Abel, and killed him. Then the LORD said to Cain, "Where is Abel your brother?" He said, "I do not know; am I my brother's keeper?" And the LORD said, "What have you done? The voice of your brother's blood is crying to me from the ground. And now you are cursed from the ground, which has opened its mouth to receive your brother's blood from your hand. When you till the ground, it shall no longer yield to you its strength; you shall be a fugitive and a wanderer on the earth." Cain said to the LORD, "My punishment is greater than I can bear. Behold, thou hast driven me this day away from the ground; and from thy face I shall be hidden; and I shall be a fugitive and a wanderer on the earth, and whoever finds me will slay me." (Genesis 4:8-14)

Cain robbed Abel of his future by murdering him, leaving his body to bleed in a field. In murdering his brother, Cain also gave up his own future and hope. Implicit in Cain's plea in verse 14 is the recognition that the penalty for murder is death, just as will be formalized in law codes later in the Torah (see Exodus 21:12). Cain recognizes his own perilous situation and loses hope for his own future. He knows that he will be driven from the ground and hidden from God's face. He will be a fugitive and a wanderer, liable to be killed by anyone he might meet. He has no future and no hope.

God himself steps in to make a difference. Even to the murderer, a future is granted by the imposition of God's own mark: "Then the LORD said to him, 'Not so! If any one slays Cain, vengeance shall be taken on him sevenfold.' And the LORD put a mark on Cain, lest any who came upon him should kill him" (Genesis 4:15). We are not told of any mitigating circumstance or any special merit that Cain might have earned. The granting of a future and a hope is all God's doing—apparently because God takes delight in the work of his hands.

Flood Narrative

The Flood story may seem like a strange place to look for hope. A careful examination of the story, however, will find that hope concludes the story and propels us on to the future.

The story begins ominously. God regrets making humanity and determines to do something about it. "The LORD saw that the wickedness of man was great in the earth, and that every imagination of the thoughts of his heart was only evil continually" (6:5). Yet even here, the future is not wiped out, for a family is chosen on which the future will be built. Despite the pain that sinful humanity had caused to God, the threat of complete eradication is removed, and a new future is promised:

> And the LORD was sorry that he had made man on the earth, and it grieved him to his heart. So the LORD said, "I will blot out man whom I have created from the face of the ground, man and beast and creeping things and birds of the air, for I am sorry that I have made them." But Noah found favor in the eyes of the LORD. (6:6-8)

From that point on, the story is well known. Noah is convinced to build a great ship. The selected animals are loaded onboard; and for days Noah, his family, and his precious cargo of future life ride out the storm as everything else on earth is literally washed away. What is sometimes overlooked, however, is a very deliberate post-Flood evaluation that God makes of the whole situation. Using the very same words that God used back in Genesis 6:5 when the whole episode began, God again evaluates the condition of humanity: "I will never again curse the ground because of man, for the imagination of man's heart is evil from his youth; neither will I ever again destroy every living creature as I have done" (8:21b).

Nothing has changed. Humanity is still separate from God and still makes God grieve, still makes God heartbroken or sick to death. What has changed is that now hope is prominent. Apparently, God chose to bear the heartbreak of humanity-gone-bad, rather than totally annihilate the work of his hands. God chose to offer hope.

The Tower of Babel

The story of the tower of Babel is relatively short, taking only nine verses at the beginning of Genesis 11. The story follows hard upon the heels of the Flood story and the description of Noah's descendants. The danger present at the Flood is the backdrop for the telling of the tower story. We are told that the people's motivation for making the tower was to "make a name for ourselves" and to prevent being "scattered abroad" (11:4). In other words, the tower was to be a tower of hope, a way to find security in the face of an uncertain future. However, God intervenes, and humanity is dispersed. A false hope is removed, and the stage is set for a better hope, one effective and available to all.

The Call of Abraham

In Genesis 12:1-3, and in contrast to the gathered strength of humanity in chapter 11, Abram, whom God will later call Abraham, is called by God away from his family and all that is familiar to him. In contrast to the human ingenuity and inventiveness expressed in the tower of Babel, the Abraham story moves along on God's initiative alone. Further, it is clear that this story involves not just the private dealings of one man and God, but rather something is afoot in this episode that will affect all the families of the earth.

> Now the LORD said to Abram, "Go from your country and your kindred and your father's house to the land that I will show you. And I will make of you a great nation, and I will bless you, and make your name great, so that you will be a blessing. I will bless those who bless you, and him who curses you I will curse; and by you all the families of the earth shall bless themselves." (12:1-3)

A blessing is in store. To this point, the curses for which a blessing is needed, and which have been applied to all humanity, take us back to the garden of Eden and chapter 3 of Genesis. These curses had to do with death and with the loss of future and hope. A blessing, equally applied—at least potentially—to all humanity, can be expected to undo that curse, and to affect the remedy of that loss of hope and future.

And this is exactly what we find. This restoration of future and hope is stated in terms that would be immediately plain to ancient readers from the Near East. The blessing that God brought to Abraham was heaped in terms of land and descendants: "Then the LORD appeared to Abram, and said, 'To your descendants I will give this land' " (12:7a).

Both land and descendants provided tangible and practical evidence of a future and a hope. These same two gifts are present whenever God deals with Abraham (Genesis 13:14 and following; 15; 17:1-2; 24:7-8). The same promise is extended to Abraham's immediate descendants—to Isaac:

> Sojourn in this land, and I will be with you, and will bless you; for to you and to your descendants I will give all these lands, and I will fulfil the oath which I swore to Abraham your father. I will multiply your descendants as the stars of the heaven, and will give to your descendants all these lands; and by your descendants all the nations of the earth shall bless themselves. (26:3-4)

and to Jacob:

> And behold, the LORD stood above it and said, "I am the LORD, the God of Abraham your father and the God of Isaac; the land on which you lie I will give to you and to your descendants; and your descendants shall be like the dust of the earth, and you shall spread abroad to the west and to the east and to the north and to the south; and by you and your descendants shall all the families of the earth bless themselves." (28:13-14)

Like a thread running through the last half of Genesis, a future hope is present whenever God appears. Hope is present, not just for Abraham and his family, but hope is near for all the families of the earth. Consistently in all these dealings between God and the family of Abraham, the real goal is a blessing applied to all humanity. Abraham and his family are like conduits that are used to bring a supply of hope and future to all touched by the curse of death and pain.

Exodus

In the Book of Exodus we leave behind the patriarchs, Abraham and his near descendants, and enter a new chapter in the story. Still, however, a forward orientation is maintained, and hope is present. The whole Exodus event—the Hebrews' release from slavery in Egypt, their wanderings in the wilderness, and their entry into the Promised Land—is built upon a memory and a hope:

> In the course of those many days the king of Egypt died. And the people of Israel groaned under their bondage, and cried out for help, and their cry under bondage came up to God. And God heard their groaning, and God remembered his covenant with Abraham, with Isaac, and with Jacob. And God saw the people of Israel, and God knew their condition. (Exodus 2:23-25)

Everything that happens in the story of the Exodus, from this point on, is all built upon these three verses. It's all a result of God acting upon the promise of hope that he extended to Abraham and his family. The same idea is repeated in the next chapter (3:7, 17), and the Promised Land clearly comes into focus. The hope present in the Creation account gives way to the hope given by God to the patriarchs, who in turn make way for the expression of hope extended to all Israel in the Exodus. The journey to the future (a land of promise) dominates the rest of the Torah.

Hope is a dominant characteristic of the way that God interacts with people all through the Torah. The fulfillment of that hope is always and only dependent upon the faithfulness of God. There is no special righteousness evident in Cain or Abraham or Isaac or Jacob. The Israelites are no more upright than their Egyptian neighbors. And even Moses gets fed up with the people he is to lead, as well as with God (see Numbers 11:10-15). No, the future is available because of God alone.

Balaam

God's sole ownership of the future is a point that bears special emphasis and is driven home by a fascinating little story buried in the middle of the Book of Numbers, chapters 22–24. In the story, the Israelites are making their way slowly but steadily toward the Promised Land. Word has spread of God's miraculous intervention to lead the Israelites through the Red Sea to safety and freedom, to defeat the mighty Egyptian army, and to bring a devastating victory over the combined forces of the Amorites, causing fear among all the surrounding peoples.

Balak, king of the Moabite peoples and himself fearful of the Israelite might, enlists the help of Balaam to confound the future of the Israelites. The Israelites are headed for the Promised Land, and Balak, with Balaam's help, wants to do everything he can to prevent that. Balaam is a man of remarkable talents, mentioned both in the Bible and in other pieces of literature from the ancient Near East (*Writings From Ancient Israel: A Handbook of Historical and Religious Documents*, by Klaas A. D. Smelik, translated by G. I. Davies; Westminster John Knox, 1991; pages 79–92). His reputation is known far and wide. Behind Balak's request is the belief that a person—indeed, a very special person like Balaam—can determine the future. In Balak's own words addressed to Balaam, "For I know that he whom you bless is blessed, and he whom you curse is cursed" (Numbers 22:6b).

But Balak could not be more wrong; for as the story shows, the future belongs solely to God. First, Balaam is confronted by his own inability when faced with the exclusive rights of God: "Balaam said to Balak, 'Lo, I have come to you! Have I now any power at all to speak anything? The word that God puts in my mouth, that must I speak'" (22:38).

And then Balak, too, must recognize that the future belongs only to God, and that hope must be a gift received from God's hand (24:15-17).

What Balaam and Balak learned, through tragedy, can become a valuable and helpful lesson for the rest of us. The future belongs only to God. The whole Torah is bound together by this one theme. Inevitably, whenever and wherever God is present, there, too, hope is present; for God is the future-generating and future-sustaining God.

Names of God

Even this brief survey of the Torah would be incomplete if we didn't take just a little time to examine the way God is characterized by means of the Hebrew names given to him throughout the Torah. Throughout the Old Testament, and particularly in the Torah, the names used for God are important indicators of the real character of God (*The Anchor Bible Dictionary*, Vol. 4, edited by David Noel Freedman; Doubleday, 1992; pages 1001–11). To the common designation for the Deity in the Hebrew Bible, *Elohim* (אלהים), translated in English as "God," several other names are added. The names for God do more than label God. These names provide a means of access to God. For example, the name "Dad," more a title or descriptive of a relationship, implies a means of access to those who have the right to use the name. There are three and only three people in all the universe who have the right and effective ability to address me in this manner. They have a special means of access to me. So, too, those who have been given the right to use the following names for God have a distinctive access to God. As means of access to God, these names give some insight into the vision of hope in the Old Testament.

Yahweh (יהוה), LORD

The place to begin to understand this name in the Old Testament is Exodus 3. In the opening chapters of Exodus, the reader has been confronted by the hopeless condition of the children of Israel under Egyptian oppression. Moses, the supposed agent of rescue, has just fled the country and is a fugitive hiding under the cloak of a shepherd in the middle of a wild and barren wasteland. He is presented with a spectacle, a bush burning but not consumed by the flames, which draws his attention for a closer look. If located on the side of a mountain, anywhere near what is traditionally believed to be the site of this encounter, this flaming bush could have been seen, at night at least, for miles around. Moses' detour to investigate the light glowing may have taken him a journey of several days.

In dramatic and totally unexpected fashion, Moses meets more than a fiery bush. Moses meets God and receives from God a commission to return to Egypt to secure the freedom of the Israelite slaves. Wanting some guarantee of God's power and presence while on this unlikely journey, Moses asks God his name. The reply is, "I am Yahweh." Often translated "I AM WHO I AM" or "I cause to be," the personal name of God appearing here is some form of the verb "to be" and communicates God's unique relationship to being both now and in the future. This name is more than a convenient label; as Exodus 3:15 suggests, it is a way of accessing the Creator: "God also said to Moses, 'Say this to the people of Israel, "The LORD [Yahweh], the God of your fathers, the God of Abraham, the God of Isaac, and the God of Jacob, has sent me to you": this is my name for ever, and thus I am to be remembered throughout all generations.' "

One way of translating the name Yahweh that I have found to be evident, especially in my reading of Moses' experience, is "The Self-Determined One." God's answer to Moses comes at just the right time and in just the right circumstance. Faced with a very unlikely future—Moses is a wanted criminal in Egypt, and the Hebrew slaves appear to be in no position to mount a successful revolt—Moses comes to know God as the One who holds the future in his hand. Based upon God's exclusive possession of the future, God can also unconditionally claim self-determination. God will be in the future just what God chooses. Upon this unshakable foundation, God is able to offer Moses hope for his future as well.

Exodus 6:2-3 adds a bit more to our understanding: "And God said to Moses, 'I am the LORD. I appeared to Abraham, to Isaac, and to Jacob, as God Almighty, but by my name the LORD I did not make myself known to them.'" Here, God indicates that previously he was known by the patriarchs, Abraham, Isaac, and Jacob, as *El Shaddai* (Almighty), but now God is also to be known as *Yahweh* (the LORD). The combination of the two names is quite powerful. God is the "Provider," a loose sense of what *shaddai* means, and is able to offer needed provision to those whom God will (*The New Brown, Driver, Briggs, Gesenius: Hebrew and English Lexicon*, by Francis Brown; Hendrickson, 1979; pages 994–95). God is also the One who governs and who calls into being the future—God is also *Yahweh*.

El Shaddai (אל שׁרי), Almighty God

In Genesis 17:1 God tells Abram that by this name, God Almighty, Abram has access to the Deity: "When Abram was ninety-nine years old the LORD appeared to Abram, and said to him, 'I am God Almighty; walk before me, and be blameless.'"

El Shaddai calls Abram into a relationship with him and repeats the promises that were made in Genesis 12. Chief among those promises are descendants and land:

> Behold, my covenant is with you, and you shall be the father of a multitude of nations. No longer shall your name be Abram, but your name shall be Abraham; for I

have made you the father of a multitude of nations. I will make you exceedingly fruitful; and I will make nations of you, and kings shall come forth from you. And I will establish my covenant between me and you and your descendants after you throughout their generations for an everlasting covenant, to be God to you and to your descendants after you. (Genesis 17:4-7)

Thus, the name *El Shaddai* functions as guarantee of that promise-bearing future.

Interestingly, the new name for God is accompanied by a name change for Abram (which means "exalted ancestor") to Abraham (meaning "ancestor of a multitude"). Sarai, his wife, also receives a new name—Sarah (although both names seem to be variants of one word meaning "princess") (*Genesis: A Commentary*, by Gerhard Von Rad; Westminster, 1972; page 202). A new way to access God meant a change in Abraham and Sarah. At some fundamental level, they became different people, presumably because they had a different relationship to the future and the source of hope.

The remainder of the times that this name for God, *El Shaddai*, is used in Genesis (28:3; 35:11; 43:14; 48:3; 49:25) all have to do with the formation of a similar covenant with the succeeding generations of Abraham's family, or it is found in a blessing that one generation pronounces upon the next. *El Shaddai* has the ability to shape the future according to promises made in the present.

Yahweh Roeh [Jehovah Jireh] (יהוה יראה), The LORD Sees

We meet God, "The LORD sees," in Genesis 22: "So Abraham called the name of that place The LORD will provide [The LORD sees]; as it is said to this day, 'On the mount of the LORD it shall be provided' " (22:14, adapted).

This name is a proclamation made by Abraham upon the miraculous rescue of Isaac, his son, following the near sacrifice on Mount Moriah. God who Sees (אל ראי), a variant of the name, appears earlier in Genesis 16:13: "So she called the name of the LORD who spoke to her, 'Thou art a God of seeing.'"

Here in Genesis 16, Hagar, following God's rescue of her from Sarai's mistreatment, gives this name for God in gratitude and awe. Immediately following the name we are given the birth announcement of Hagar's son, Ishmael (verses 15-16). It is significant that both of the offspring of Abraham, Isaac and Ishmael (through Hagar, his mother), experience rescues in which God is present as the "God who sees." A future is given to all of Abraham's descendants, not based upon their merit but based solely upon the person of God.

El Olam (אל צולם), Everlasting God

In the Book of Genesis, this name appears only once: "Abraham planted a tamarisk tree in Beer-sheba, and called there on the name of the LORD, the Everlasting God" (Genesis 21:33).

The name "Everlasting God" is given by Abraham upon the successful negotiation of rights to wells in the vicinity of Beer-sheba. This name is in honor of the life-giving provision of water that God has made for Abraham in a very parched and dry place. Those wells were seen as gifts of life from the Everlasting God. The joy of the moment given expression in Genesis 21 also may have been captured by Isaiah, writing at a much later date, in his use of the same name for God:

> Have you not known? Have you not heard?
> The LORD is the everlasting God,
>   the Creator of the ends of the earth.
> He does not faint or grow weary;
>   his understanding is unsearchable.
> He gives power to the faint,
>   and strengthens the powerless.
> Even youths will faint and be weary,

and the young will fall exhausted;
but those who wait [hope] for the LORD shall renew their
   strength,
they shall mount up with wings like eagles,
they shall run and not be weary,
they shall walk and not faint.

(Isaiah 40:28-31, NRSV, adapted)

Wings are given to *us* as well—to all those who hope in the LORD, the Everlasting God, Creator of heaven and earth.

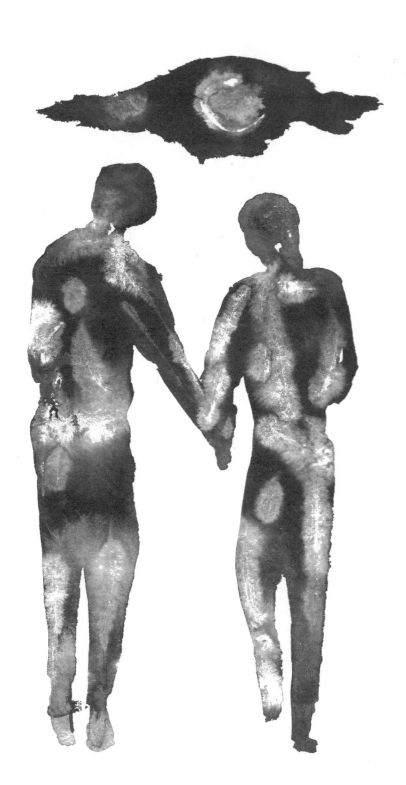

PART 3:

THE JOURNEY ON

10

HEAVEN IS WHERE YOU ARE

THE LAST SEVERAL CHAPTERS of this book have been spent in surveying, what have become for me, key passages in the Old Testament describing God as our hope, our future, and our portion. Our doubter's guide to heaven has been leading us to God. But the information about God is not enough. It isn't information about God that produces hope, but rather God himself. We must encounter the living God if we are to face the future with confidence. If we are to be functional, to live skillfully, we will do so in the presence of God. This chapter tells a story that I trust will point us in the direction of living in God's presence.

I spent the late spring and summer of 1991 in Addis Ababa, Ethiopia. Although both the people and the country were wonderful, the timing for my visit was horrible. Ethiopia was in the throes of a civil war; and the capital, Addis Ababa, was under siege and then overrun. Most of the foreigners had long since left the country, and those of us who remained were alternately objects of mistrust, protection, and hope. Mostly, we were treated well by all sides in the conflict. In the period between the flight of the national security forces and the occupation of the rebel forces from the north, the city was left in a state of bewilderment, with everyone collectively holding his or her breath, not knowing what would come next.

Actually, the transition went much more smoothly than it could have. A dusk-to-dawn curfew was strictly enforced, but even then, running gun battles interspersed by the report of larger 50mm-machine-gun and tank fire were nightly occurrences throughout the city. Parts of the city were heavily damaged (the local Pepsi bottling plant was a total loss, much to the dismay of everyone on both sides of the conflict), while other parts of the city were hardly touched by the effects of the fighting. As you might imagine, the infrastructure of the city and services were interrupted and curtailed. Water and electricity were sporadic, as were travel and the supply of food stores.

One of the most notable hardships was the scarcity of kerosene. June and July are the rainy months in Addis, and kerosene is used for its limited warmth but mostly for cooking. The equation is easy: no kerosene, no food—and so this cooking fuel became a much valued commodity, and at times people became quite desperate to acquire some.

Particularly hard-hit by the shortage were the slum areas of the city, packed with people and only very poorly provided with water or sewage services. On one particular occasion, I witnessed a mob gathering at a petrol station, which was being guarded by a few of the rebel soldiers. (The term "soldier" is used loosely; many of these were only boys, some no older than fifteen, dressed in ragged clothes and very unsure of themselves.) The people came with old coffee cans, water pots, anything that might be used as a container in which to hold some of the precious fuel. At first the soldiers beat back the mob with lengths of rubber hoses, much like garden hoses that people use to water their lawns. When that failed to be an effective deterrent, shots were scattered in the air overhead. When even that couldn't keep the people back from the pumps, three of the soldiers leveled their weapons and fired into the crowd. People ran in all directions, except for the six I counted lying there on the pavement. Unfortunately, this kind of thing was not rare at all.

I fell into the habit of walking around the city early in the morning, after curfew was over but before the rains began. It really wasn't a very smart thing to do, but if I was careful and kept my wits about me, I could manage to steer clear of trouble—most of the time.

It was fascinating to watch the city awaken, and I tried to walk in different directions each day. A lot of people slept on the streets, some in cardboard and tin shelters, many with no shelter at all. Leprosy (also known as Hansen's disease) was much too frequent there, and many, many of those on the streets were afflicted by this hideous catalogue of disease. I passed a lot of these people on my walks.

Workers driving around the city in flatbed trucks were also my frequent companions. At first I assumed they were trash collectors, for in the distance, I could see the trucks stop, then men would jump off to the side of the road and throw something up into the truck. They would then drive off a bit further down the road and repeat the whole process again and again. It wasn't until I happened close to one of the trucks that the true nature of their grisly business dawned on me: These men were not loading garbage onto their trucks, but bodies of people who had died during the night. It was a macabre and terrible dance that was performed every morning when the day awoke.

I'll never forget rounding a corner on one of my morning walks and coming upon a pack of dogs that had found someone before the men in the flatbed truck had arrived. When the dogs spied me, the pack scattered, each carrying in its mouth as much as it could and leaving behind a barely recognizable form. A casualty of cruelty, disease, and death, now nameless and all but forgotten. The war had exacted a heavy price from many people, reducing them to little more than food for the dogs.

Death and violence were much too common that summer of 1991. But no less so were heroism, kindness, and simple acts of generosity. One man, whom I have come to respect very much, invited me to his home, a tin hut no larger than eight feet by ten feet, and lit by a single dangling bulb attached to a bare wire. He made coffee for me and prayed for me. He gave me all he had, and little did he know its true worth.

I made some good friends in that place that summer, friends who taught me a lot about faith and thankfulness. There was a place not far from where I was staying that passed for a coffee shop of sorts, where you could sit on some old, cracked and broken resin chairs and sip chai tea from chipped glasses. Conversations, often sprinkled by the crack of gunfire, there on those chairs are some of my best memories from that violent time and place.

Every day, I wrote letters home to my wife and children. Most of the letters made it home, and many of them are now stuffed in an old shoebox. I know where the letters are but have not once looked at them since they were written those years ago. Some of the memories of that time and place I simply do not want to resurrect. At the time, however, those letters were a real godsend. Actually, it was the act of writing the letters that was the real benefit. Once a day, I could set aside time to turn my attention to those I loved in the life that I left those weeks and months before. Those letters became my connection to a life that I had left, a life I longed to reenter.

I do remember that as I wrote, a sure and growing joy was imprinted in me at the thought of seeing my family again. Each day that passed brought the reunion one day closer and made me just a little more impatient. As the time for my return inched closer, it was all I could think about. Addis to Cairo to Amsterdam to Toronto; the flight seemed unending.

At last the plane landed, the doors were opened, and I was led through the airport to a waiting car, which would take me to where I would be greeted by a longed-for embrace in Cher's arms. And finally—there she was! I don't think I've ever been happier than I was at that moment. She was there, and that's what made it special.

That last sentence is the catch, and the point, of this chapter: Just as my wife's presence made the place of our reunion special, so too it is the presence of God that makes heaven special. Heaven is where God is. But, *where* is a God who is everywhere present?

That is exactly the point that Jesus seems to be making when, in the parables, he talks about the kingdom of God, likening it to a mustard seed that is growing unnoticed and silent, right there in front of you, until one day it is so big and so obvious that even passing birds can't resist it (Matthew 13:31-32; Mark 4:30-32). Again, as Jesus said, "The kingdom of God is not coming with things that can be observed.... For, in fact, the kingdom of God is among you" (Luke 17:20b-21, NRSV).

Apparently, the kingdom of God—heaven—is present, to some degree at least, here and now. But if that is so, then it is present for me to *experience* here and now, and my thoughts of deferring the enjoyment of heaven until some future time may in fact lead me to miss out on some of that "reunion joy" that God has in store for me now. Could it be that there is actually the possibility that I can experience heaven now, and that *experience* is the very best proof that there is more to come? Maybe the future experience of heaven is an intensification of the kind of experience that we have available to us now. Perhaps heaven isn't a place different in kind so much as it is an experience different in intensity.

If this reasoning is at all sound, then our guide to heaven will miss the point if it doesn't include a consideration of our quality of life here and now. It's as if the future invades the present. Heaven works itself back into our here and now. Could that be the reason why the apostle Paul was eventually able to declare that he was learning to be content in every circumstance (Philippians 4:11)? Could Paul see a glimpse of heaven no matter where he was?

11

NEITHER HERE NOR THERE

DOUBT RESULTS WHEN THE OLD paradigms, the old ways of looking at things, simply don't work any longer. For me, personal crisis convinced me that my old way of looking at things—and my way of looking at God, in particular—simply wouldn't do. But there are other reasons why doubt emerges. All around us there are cultural forces sweeping across the landscape that have tremendous implications for the way in which spiritual knowledge is articulated. There is a religious reformation occurring that is casting a shadow of doubt over the way in which spiritual realities have been described even within the last half-century. "The old" simply will not do anymore. The change in religious thinking taking place currently may very well rival those changes that led to the Protestant Reformation of the sixteenth century.

As a college teacher, I see it all the time. The generation coming of age at the turn of the millennium no longer makes a strong connection between religion and spirituality. For many of these people, religion and spirituality are two different things. In general terms, this group of people, growing exponentially in numbers, considers themselves very spiritual but at the same time very distrusting of religious forms. In other words, the religious forms are, for many in this group, no longer sufficient in addressing their spiritual needs or concerns. When customary ways of thinking and speaking about spiritual realities become insufficient, religious doubt results.

This sort of thing has happened before. In the history of the Judeo-Christian tradition, religious reformations—that is, changes in the way spiritual realities are known and perceived—have always been accompanied by changes in people's perception of space and location. When people think differently about their place in the world, or in the cosmos, they think differently about God and use different words to express a relationship to him. For example, the Protestant Reformation led by Martin Luther and John Calvin was accompanied by a new awareness, continuing discovery, and exploration of the New World. The idea that Europe, and particularly Rome, was the center of the human universe simply would no longer fly. People saw their own location differently. They saw their own space with new eyes, and the boundaries of the spiritual universe were upset no less than the boundaries of the physical world.

The *Pax Romana* ("Roman Peace"), or the period of domination of the Roman Empire over the Mediterranean Basin, changed the perception of space and location for those living in this region at from the first century B.C.E. to at least the second century C.E. Particularly for those living in Ancient Palestine and accustomed to thinking of themselves as the center of God's kingdom, the Roman Empire shattered all the accepted boundaries between peoples and lands (*From Revelation to Canon: Studies in the Hebrew Bible and Second Temple Literature*, by James C. Vanderkam; Brill Academic Publishers, 2000; pages 492–99). Caesar's kingdom and the New Testament kingdom of God were no longer determined by ethnic boundaries, with the result being that the good news of Jesus Christ was proclaimed to both Jew and Gentile.

The first eight verses of the Book of Acts are a striking example of this startling change. The disciples ask the resurrected Jesus about the kingdom of God, expecting that it would soon be restored to Israel. Jesus responds in an unexpected fashion, declaring that the kingdom of God is no longer limited to Israel and those of Jewish descent, but extends to the "end of the earth" and is peopled by those from every nation.

The same holds true in the pre-Christian Israelite tradition as well, at least as it is represented in the Old Testament. There, too, is evidence of a connection between religious reformations and changes in the people's awareness of space and location. Probably the best-known change of location that occurs in the Old Testament is the Exodus of the Israelite slaves from Egypt. As the Israelites journeyed from Egypt, making their way to a Promised Land, they took a roundabout route lasting a number of years. All the while, a portable tabernacle, or place of worship, in which the presence of God was believed to be localized, was carried along with them. As the people of Israel moved, God moved too by means of this portable focus of his Presence (Exodus 25–27; 36–38).

But this new way of thinking about God involved more than simply a movable place to worship. Moses' burning bush experience in Exodus 3 makes clear that the change in Israelite worldview was accompanied by the use of a new name for God: *Yahweh* (LORD). Exodus 6:2-3 gives the impression that this really was a religious reformation that was taking place as the Israelites changed their location and their place in the world. In the course of their journey, the Israelites were led to Mount Sinai, and there they received the Ten Commandments, or Decalogue. This famous set of moral norms is presented two times in the biblical text, and both times the statement "I am the LORD your God, who brought you out of the land of Egypt, out of the house of bondage" (Exodus 20:2; Deuteronomy 5:6) serves as a preamble. God's name, *Yahweh*, serves as an introductory reminder that a new way of life was the expected outcome of this new spiritual awareness. A dramatic relocation to the promised land served as the occasion for a revolutionary religious reform.

Likewise, at the other end of the Old Testament story, a change in space and location expressed itself in a changed understanding of God. The destruction of Jerusalem and the exile of the Israelite community into Babylon was, in the books of the prophets, given expression as an enlarged view of God. No longer the Lord God of Israel or the tribal God of Judah, the prophets expressed their understanding of God as sovereign over all humanity (Isaiah 19:19-24; 37:20; 49:6; Habakkuk 3:3; see also *History and Prophecy: The Development of Late Judean Literary Traditions*, by Brian Peckham; Doubleday, 1993). The exile into Babylon made the localized concentration on Palestine no longer sufficient. The world had suddenly gotten a whole lot bigger—and the people's understanding of God got bigger too. In the books of the prophets, we find statements about God's involvement in the affairs of a variety of people groups. Even the Exodus from Egypt, the hallmark of Israel's "chosen" status, is replicated in the experience of others: " 'Are you not like the Ethiopians to me, O people of Israel?' says the LORD. 'Did I not bring up Israel from the land of Egypt, and the Philistines from Caphtor and the Syrians from Kir?' " (Amos 9:7). Other peoples had Exodus-like experiences with God too!

God's sovereign care for all peoples, even Israel's enemies, becomes a major theme in the books of the prophets: "In that day Israel will be the third with Egypt and Assyria, a blessing in the midst of the earth, whom the LORD of hosts has blessed, saying, 'Blessed be Egypt my people, and Assyria the work of my hands, and Israel my heritage' " (Isaiah 19:24-25).

This thumbnail sketch outlining moments of intense religious and geographic change is simply a prelude to say that we, too, are once again in a moment in which space and distance are changing, and so too must our talk about heaven. Let me see if I can explain what I mean.

We live in a world in which neither here nor there matters anymore. Distance, space, and location are being erased in two seemingly contradictory ways. First, "there" no longer matters. The Internet and its corollary communication technologies have effectively erased the distance between people so that "there" has lost much of its meaning in human discourse. I need no longer be in close physical proximity to "reach out and touch someone."

This fact of change was brought home to me in a powerful fashion. My son, like many high-school- and college-age people, enjoys Internet games and the chat rooms that often go along with the games. One evening, I sat down next to him at the computer and was utterly amazed at something that he and his generation take for granted. He was playing an online game that incorporated a "chat box"—a real-time dialogue mechanism between the players. The players could play the game and type notes to each other at the same time. What amazed me was where these other players lived: Moscow, London, Atlanta, Sydney (at that hour, that guy should have been in bed!), and Western Pennsylvania were the addresses of my son's online game companions. The neighborhood sure isn't what it used to be! When I was a teenager, "over there" or "too far" meant about five blocks away. For my son, neighborhood companions span the globe. The concept of "there" as being beyond reach or utterly disconnected no longer exists.

But "here" is pretty meaningless too. One evening several months ago, I sat in our family room watching a TV show in sheer amazement. The show was about the Hubble Space Telescope. I'll acknowledge my guilt right away: I am totally fascinated by the idea of space exploration; and the images captured by the Hubble telescope, then being broadcast on TV, captivated me. But what I found most amazing were not the images themselves, but the distances. The narrator of the TV show explained that the telescope was picking up images of objects 17 billion light years away. That number is way too big for me to really comprehend, except by saying that we live in a really big, big place.

Seventeen billion light years—and that's just looking off in one direction. The universe is huge, and we are just beginning to understand what this means. Think about this for a moment. According to *The American Heritage Dictionary*, the sun is about 93 million miles away from the earth (fourth edition online, Houghton Mifflin Company, 2000). It only takes about eight minutes for light to reach us from the sun; only *eight minutes* to travel *93 million miles*! Imagine how far light travels in one hour (about 7.2 times 93 million). Or ask yourself, how far does light go in a day, or a week, or a month, or even a year—and now multiply that last figure by 17 billion. Copernicus taught us that we are not the center of the universe, much less the center of our own little solar system (*The American Heritage Dictionary*, 2000). The Hubble telescope shows us not only that we are not the center of the universe but that we are not even a tiny speck in this immense and vast expanse. In the context of a place that is more than 17 billion light years huge, "here" hardly matters at all.

So you have it: We live in an era where neither "here" nor "there" matters. Space, distance, and location have changed in the past twenty years like no other time in all of human history. And now the question is, what does this mean about heaven? What is heaven like in a world where "here" and "there" have little meaning?

A conversation between a Samaritan woman and Jesus illustrates the spiritual consequences that result from a change in place. Toward the end of the conversation, the Samaritan woman makes a very interesting observation. She states, "Our ancestors worshiped on this mountain, but you say that the place where people must worship is in Jerusalem" (John 4:20, NRSV). From our perspective in the early twenty-first century, it might be hard to grasp the significance of this woman's statement; but in reality she was addressing one of the most central concerns that she and Jesus could share.

The conversation took place in Shechem, next to Jacob's well. This site has a long, long history of religious importance. Shechem is the location of Mount Ebal and of Mount Gerizim, the latter of which is considered a sacred place of blessing (Deuteronomy 27–28). Shechem is where Joshua brought the people of Israel to renew their covenant with God (Joshua 24). Shechem was a place of worship and a place where God frequented.

The Samaritans were convinced that Shechem was the place where God should be worshiped. Indeed, from the Samaritan point of view, God had commanded that he be worshiped there (*Tradition Kept*, by Robert T. Anderson and Terry Giles; Hendrickson, 2005; page 31). The rest of the Israelite community, however, under the direction of David and the later kings, focused on Jerusalem as the spot to build a temple and worship God. This dispute over the proper site of worship (and all of the organization and ritual that went with it) was at the very heart of the controversy between the Jews and the Samaritans (*The Keepers: An Introduction to the History and Culture of the Samaritans*, by Robert T. Anderson and Terry Giles; Hendrickson, 2002; pages 40–42). So when the woman at the well brought up the topic of where to worship, she was addressing the very central issue—*How can I worship God?* Or maybe better, *Where is God?*

To all of this, Jesus' response is important for us: "Woman, believe me, the hour is coming when you will worship the Father neither on this mountain nor in Jerusalem" (John 4:21, NRSV). Essentially, Jesus replies that neither here nor there is the place of worship. But if you go further, Jesus indicates that worship is not about place at all. It isn't *where* you worship but *how*: "God is spirit, and those who worship him must worship in spirit and truth" (4:24, NRSV).

Jesus is literally breaking all the boundaries. This is where it gets interesting. If worship brings us into the presence of God, and if worship isn't about a place, then God must not be in a place either. And if God is not in a place, then heaven (where God is) isn't about place. Space or location may no longer be useful ways of talking about heaven. I don't *go* to heaven when I die; heaven *envelops* me. Heaven is a way of being, not a place in which to be.

Think of heaven in a fashion similar to a love relationship. I am *in* love with my wife. By that statement, I don't mean that I am at a place where I love my wife. When I say I am *in* love, I don't mean a place at all, as I would if I were to say I am *in* town or *in* the car. *In love* indicates a way that I *am*, not a place. *In love* indicates that everything about me has been affected—my thoughts, my emotions, my attitudes, my likes and dislikes, everything has changed because I am *in* love. Being in love is not being in a place, but it is a way of being.

That must be how it is with heaven. Heaven is not a place, but a way of being. Jesus was fond of saying that the kingdom of God is within us (Matthew 10:7; Luke 17:21). Now, those statements make perfect sense. He didn't mean that heaven occupies a small place in my body or infects me like a virus, but rather that heaven is a way of being. Heaven is as close to me as the air I breathe, because it is a way in which I live. C. S. Lewis writes about heaven invading the present. Imagine, if you will, a lifestyle that you would expect to find of a resident of heaven. Now, consider that we are those residents. Those wondrous imaginations of heaven, according to Lewis, invade my present (*The Great Divorce*, by C. S. Lewis, in *Five Best Books In One Volume*; Baker Book House, 1969; pages 192–93).

So, all of that begs the question: What would that lifestyle look like? How does a resident of heaven live? That question will be taken up in the next few chapters.

12

I LOOKED
THROUGH THE KEYHOLE

 Does a taste of heaven *now* awaken in us a longing that, in turn, provides evidence of more to come? In the early months of my wife's illness, we talked often of heaven. Unlike me, she was filled with confidence and was never plagued by the doubts that assailed me. I envied her and wondered at the nature of her confidence, yet wanted to do nothing to upset her surety by revealing my own nagging questions. As is often the case, however, she figured out what was troubling me and frequently assumed the role of confidante and teacher, allowing me to come to her with my deepest concerns. When finally I mustered up the courage to ask her why she felt so confident of heaven, she replied simply and directly: "I looked through the keyhole." She had peeked through the keyhole in the door to heaven and had a glimpse of the other side.

Never one to be satisfied with the simple and direct, I asked Cher what she meant. "It's rather simple," she said. "There have been several times in my life when I have experienced overwhelming joy for which I can find no immediate cause." She explained that the joy was not self-induced, nor was it attributable to any cause that could be observed. It had to come from somewhere or someone, and she had concluded it was the result of passing close to the kingdom of heaven—she looked through the keyhole.

I think there is something to this. Cher's confidence was not placed in a set of assertions about heaven, but in an experienced reality that awoke a response deep within her. She was "functioning" in response to her environment, physical and spiritual, in a way that was consistent with the manner in which she was created. She was made—it is part of her very being—to respond positively to heaven.

It's actually not all that unusual, when you think about it. Most everything has conditions or circumstances in which it functions better than at other times or circumstances. My lawn mower functions better when the tank is filled with gas rather than with honey, even though there isn't anything inherently wrong with honey. It simply doesn't work well in my lawn mower. So, too, we function better when, in the words of the writer of Romans 15, "the God of hope fill[s] you with all joy and peace in believing, so that by the power of the Holy Spirit you may abound in hope" (15:13, adapted).

But notice, the joy referenced in Romans 15, just like the experience related by my wife, is not self-induced. Neither you nor I can wish this joy into existence, nor can we manufacture it in any other way. Apparently, the source of the joy is God himself, and no substitute will have quite the same effect. How, then, can we make ourselves susceptible to this joyful encounter with God?

In another book found in the New Testament, readers are urged to "set your minds on things that are above, not on things that are on earth. For you have died, and your life is hid with Christ in God. When Christ who is our life appears, then you also will appear with him in glory" (Colossians 3:2-4).

Following this admonition to begin realizing the reality of heaven, the reader is encouraged to begin living in accord with heaven's reality. Ethical behaviors inconsistent with the kingdom of heaven are to be avoided, and behaviors that are normative in a paradise with God are to be adopted now. As a result, peace and an awareness of the near presence of God become part of our way of life. A resonance occurs, awakening that deep God-echo within us and confirming the reality of hope in heaven. We become functional at a very deep level: "Let the peace of Christ rule in your hearts.... Let the word of Christ dwell in you richly" (3:15-16a).

In other words, we are granted glimpses through the keyhole. And notice, just like the joy given by God mentioned in Romans 15, this peace and the nearness of God are not self-induced or wish-fulfillment experiences, but are generated by God—byproducts, as it were, of functioning as intended by the Creator.

And so our functionality test ("you will know them by their fruits") can be applied to glimpses of heaven now—to "keyhole moments." The point being, put it to the test. If indeed you were made for heaven and function better mindful of the hope provided to you by the Creator, there ought to be keyhole moments confirming the correctness of your path.

My own keyhole experience has been quite different. I have been mourning my wife's mortality. Her cancer diagnosis has forced me to confront her mortality and will not let me escape the fact of a present danger. It has been a bitter cup. It has been a grief complete. But now, having drained the cup, I am discovering a hidden joy. For those given the gift of love, pain and grief are common companions. The pleasure of close company with the person you love must also know the grief of separation. When you find in another what makes you complete, you risk the threat of being pulled asunder when separation comes—and separation is inevitable. Love and grief are partners in a lifelong dance.

Most of us are destined to mourn the loss of love's fulfillment too late, when nothing is to be done about it. I, on the other hand, have been given a great gift. I have been allowed to mourn love's loss while she is still here—while there is time to perfect the love by its constant enjoyment. I have been given the great gift of urgency. I now know that life is fleeting and not to be squandered. What a great and wonderful gift has been showered on me! Having drained the cup of grief, I am now free to love fully. I can now relate to the psalmist, who says, "So teach us to number our days / that we may get a heart of wisdom" (Psalm 90:12).

Within the Christian tradition, death is both what Christ came to conquer and the means by which he conquered. Death is our great final enemy and the means by which God redeems us to perfection. This is the great scandal of all time. Death has occasioned my greatest grief and my greatest love. Death itself, unwittingly and begrudgingly, has become my keyhole glimpse of heaven.

The death of Christ is that one moment in human history when the inconceivable has happened. An invasion from beyond nature has flashed down into nature in order to set nature on its head—to create life out of death. And what I've experienced is a glimpse of just that, life coming from death. All humanity shares myths of death's reversal—a dying god who gives greater life. Can these be nothing but shadows of the supreme moment in history when it happened—the great miracle, the Resurrection—when death gave birth to life? This great scandal has turned everything inside out. And oddly, the scandal can have measurable effects on how life is lived. That's where our doubter's guide will take us in the next chapter.

13

A SEARCH FOR A ROLE MODEL

ONE OF THE MOST DIFFICULT parts of a quest for heaven is the loneliness. Oh, don't get me wrong. Lots of people, in fact just about everybody that I know, believes that there is something more beyond the grave. But just what that something more is, or what it looks like, or how it makes a real difference in life now—not too many people are on that road.

Early on, this apparent loneliness became very discouraging to me. Particularly disheartening was the lack of help that could be found in religious sources. If religious people are concerned about heaven, few of them seem to be talking about it. Sure, there is lots of fantasy writing, and some inspirational books, and there are even television shows that talk about heaven. But for doubters, these materials just aren't very satisfying. They aren't convincingly true. Part of this problem of credibility stems from the religious reformation currently underway. Some of the older religious forms that no longer resonate have yet to be replaced by forms and ways of talking that do resonate deep within; and that gap has left many people feeling empty, often not even fully knowing why.

I recently traveled to a church to give a seminar on heaven and a doubter's guide to a group composed largely of church people, well steeped in their particular customs and theology. After one of the sessions, a woman took me aside and with tears in her eyes said something that bothered me deeply. She said that she had been a member of this particular church her whole life, active in the life of the church and fully embracing a faith in Christ. But now, facing the reality of death's nearness as she aged, she had questions she wanted to talk about, but no one with whom to talk. She went on to explain that those few times when she did try to broach her concerns, she was told, "Have faith," or, "Christians don't ask that sort of thing." Her questions made people uncomfortable, and so she kept them to herself, but her loneliness grew.

On another occasion, I was at a restaurant eating a meal with a prominent leader of a large church in town. During the meal this man drew his chair close to me, lowered his voice, and said, "There are times when I really wonder about a resurrection, and the grave scares me. But if I told anybody that, I would be removed from the church board!" For both of these people, the one place where they should have been able to go with their questions, concerns, and doubts—their church family—was the very place where they could not go.

So, where can doubters turn? Is there help for the loneliness that can often plague our journey? For me, this loneliness was one of the most difficult parts of the journey, at least early on. At times, the loneliness would turn into bitterness and resentment as I felt disappointed over and over again by people who I thought should know about these things. I needed a role model, and none was to be found.

My search led me back, eventually, to the obvious. I can still remember the early-morning quiet in my office at work, when suddenly it hit me. My role model had been there all the time, and I simply had missed it. My Bible was handy, and I quickly turned in it to Matthew 5. I became more excited as I read, as if for the very first time, and it dawned on me that there it was: The Sermon on the Mount is a statement by a person who is utterly convinced of heaven, and who has determined to order his life here and now with heaven in mind. Forget that the Sermon on the Mount is in the Bible, or that it was spoken by Jesus. Take it simply as a statement about the nature of life, and there you have it. If you want to know how to live, how to act, what to think about and what values to form, all with a firm conviction of heaven, you can do no better than the Sermon on the Mount (Matthew 5–7). And so, it's a fitting way for us to end our journey together, to draw this doubter's guide to a close by spending some time immersed in the Sermon—a true guide to heaven.

It's unmistakable. The Sermon on the Mount makes no sense unless you keep heaven in mind. Biblical scholars have long debated just how this sermon was to be understood, and opinions have run the gamut. Some believe that the Sermon is a purposeful overstatement, hyperbole, in order to get people's attention. After all, isn't it a bit extreme to pluck your eye out (Matthew 5:29) or cut off your hand (verse 30) just to keep from committing some sin? Likewise, is hatred really as bad as murder (verse 22) or lust as bad as adultery (verse 28)? Others say, no, Jesus meant just what he said—the cost of being a disciple is really, really high. If you honestly try to live by the guidelines stated in the Sermon, people will walk all over you, and it will make for a miserable time—you know, turning the other cheek, and things like that (verses 39-40). Still others take a middle road of sorts, saying that Jesus *did* mean what he said, but just that he didn't mean it for here and now. They contend that the Sermon is only meant for the kingdom of God in some distant future.

While these arguments don't get solved, they certainly do fade into the background when you understand the main point of the Sermon as this: *Live with heaven in mind.* And this seems to be exactly what Jesus was modeling. What makes the Sermon on the Mount most difficult is that it presents a value system that is hard to swallow if we are focused solely on life in the present, here on earth. If *this* is all there is, then it doesn't make a lot of sense to be happy about being persecuted (5:10) or poor (5:3). If the grave ends it all, then what's the point of laying up treasures in heaven (6:19-20)? No, the Sermon makes no sense at all if there isn't something more to come.

But if heaven is calling to us, then the Sermon is a clarion call to adjust values, priorities, behaviors, and habits with this future hope—with this *more to come* in mind. If you read the Sermon against the backdrop of heaven, it becomes a very clear statement of how to live in the here and now. Some things (*people*, primarily) will increase in value because they too inhabit that distant land. Meanwhile, other things (that is, *things*, primarily) lose their worth simply because they are recognized as passing—shadows of something much more valuable to come. The Sermon helps us recognize what is truly important in light of the future the Creator is preparing for us. The Sermon on the Mount is a doubter's guide to heaven. Let's take a brief look through it.

The Beatitudes (Matthew 5:3-12)

The Sermon on the Mount opens with a series of quick, terse, and powerful statements that describe a "blessed" or truly happy person. The thing is, these statements are just the opposite of what you would expect; they turn everything upside down. This is because they redefine the scope of life; they bring heaven into the equation.

> Blessed are the poor in spirit, for theirs is the kingdom of heaven.
> Blessed are those who mourn, for they shall be comforted.
> Blessed are the meek, for they shall inherit the earth.
> Blessed are those who hunger and thirst for righteousness, for they shall be satisfied.
> Blessed are the merciful, for they shall obtain mercy.
> Blessed are the pure in heart, for they shall see God.
> Blessed are the peacemakers, for they shall be called sons of God.
> Blessed are those who are persecuted for righteousness' sake, for theirs is the kingdom of heaven.
> (Matthew 5:3-10)

The losers become the winners. The difference is that the rules of the game changed; the difference is because of heaven. Blessed people—that is, people who are fortunate and who are functioning just as their Creator designed—live their lives mindful of heaven.

This part of the Sermon isn't the only place in the Bible where living with heaven in mind makes all the difference. In Psalm 73, the psalmist voices his bewilderment and frustration caused by the apparent prosperity of bad people. Their success doesn't seem right or just, especially when compared to the psalmist's own misfortune. He relates to us that this problem just about wore him out: "Until I went into the sanctuary of God; / then I perceived their end" (verse 17)— that is, until he put the problem in perspective of heaven. And in that perspective, the psalmist's own plight seemed altogether different. His present disappointments and heartache gave way to hope. The nearness of God gave him a glimpse of heaven, a certainty of what was to come:

> Nevertheless I am continually with you;
>   you hold my right hand.
> You guide me with your counsel,
>   and afterward you will receive me with honor.
> Whom have I in heaven but you?
>   And there is nothing on earth that I desire other than you.
> My flesh and my heart may fail,
>   but God is the strength of my heart and my portion for
>   ever. (Psalm 73:23-26, NRSV)

In Matthew 5, the opening short series of statements in the Sermon on the Mount function in the same way. They are designed to give hope to people who have no evident reason for hope. The poor, the grieving, the hungry and thirsty, those who have gotten the short end of the stick have good reason to hope, we are told—for more is on the way. Something different and far better is in store. Likewise, those who have chosen to pursue a path other than self-aggrandizement and accumulation; the merciful and the peacemakers; those who have tried to do the right thing, even at great personal expense; and those who are genuinely good people—they too have a great future in store. There is a reason to hope, for in all these cases, God himself is their portion.

The Sermon begins by assuring the reader that reality is much bigger than what can presently be seen and felt. Heaven is the essential part of the equation. And because of heaven, we can be *blessed*. It's easy to skip right over that word, but we shouldn't. It's an important window into the heart of the Sermon. The Greek word translated here as *blessed* is a multifaceted word that is hard to capture by only one English word. If you could throw together the best meanings of happy, fortunate, skillful, and content all into one word, the result would be the word *blessed* (*Theological Dictionary of the New Testament*, Vol. 4, edited by Gerhard Kittel, translated by Geoffrey W. Bromiley; Eerdmans, 1967; pages 362–70).

The word comes alive in an image rather than in a definition. I have a picture of my son hanging on the wall in my study. The photograph was taken when he was perhaps eight or nine years old. In the picture, he is doing what he loves to do, fishing, with people he loves to be with, his dad and grandpa. He has a grin on his face that couldn't possibly get any bigger. His eyes are shining, and the delight that he is enjoying is evident and is immediately shared by everyone who sees the picture; they too begin to smile.

That's what *blessed* means. Blessed is a perfect delight that comes over people when they find themselves in situations that are in harmony with how they were meant to be (a young boy fishing with his grandpa) or situations that have been remedied (those who were lame walking; those who were blind seeing).

Both ideas are found wrapped up here in the opening lines of the Sermon on the Mount. Heartaches are remedied, and harmony is restored—harmony not just between us and other people, but inner harmony too, harmony that comes when there is perfect agreement between who we are on the inside and the circumstance we find ourselves in on the outside. Not limited to one ethnic group or even one religious affiliation, the Sermon on the Mount seems to be the perfect climax of the promise given to all the families of the earth through Abraham way back in Genesis 12: "And by you all the families of the earth shall bless themselves" (verse 3b).

Blessedness can be catchy. It's attractive, and it draws people into its influence. Just like that photograph of my son with the contagious smile, people mindful of heaven place themselves in a position to experience a delight that is contagious. It seeps out and spills over anyone nearby. That contagious quality of being blessed is picked up in the next part of the Sermon.

The Salt of the Earth (Matthew 5:13-48)

Like other gifts given by God, hope works best not when it is hoarded, but when it is given away. In the next part of the Sermon on the Mount, the hope extended in the Beatitudes is turned outward to affect our way of life. Beginning in Matthew 5:13, the Sermon considers the effect that the hope of heaven might have on the way people get along with one another. Those blessed people of the first part of the Sermon, those living mindful of heaven, are "the light of the world.... Let your light so shine before men, that they may see your good works and give glory to your Father who is in heaven" (verses 14, 16). The hope of heaven described in the opening lines of the Sermon that makes people blessed is transformed into a way of living life that has a definite effect on other people. The hope of heaven, lived out, becomes a shining light. That shining-light lifestyle includes a valuation placed on other people; warnings concerning matters of lust; an encouragement of faithfulness in marriage; and an appeal for kindness, mercy, and love extended to friends, enemies, and those who would take advantage of you. These aren't the only areas of life where keeping heaven in mind can make a difference; these are only examples.

All indications point to the conclusion that the Sermon on the Mount, as it appears in Matthew, is tightly woven with each piece of the Sermon structured to powerfully communicate. The section from 5:13 to 5:48 is a series of paragraphs, each introduced by a variant of the phrase "You have heard that it was said" (see 5:21, 27, 31, 33, 38, 43), followed by a retort in which Jesus says, "But I say to you" (see 5:22, 28, 32, 34, 39, 44). The "you have heard that it was said" phrase introduces a statement of law or moral standard that everyone listening would have known quite well. It was part of the accepted religious and ethical norm that people observed. But that accepted norm is, in Jesus' opinion, not quite right; for after quoting that accepted standard he encourages his listeners to go a step higher, telling them, "But I say to you." Jesus moves beyond the norm that he quotes. *His* standard points all in one direction. He asks more of his listeners. The *more* that he asks has a common thread. One of the striking characteristics of this part of the Sermon is the way in which *people* are valued over *things*. Those living with heaven in mind value people more than they value things. It's the *people* that really matter. *People* have a future, but everything else rusts and decays away (6:19-21).

The importance of people is given expression in several examples throughout Matthew 5, one of which is rather odd and a bit counterintuitive at first. To this point, the Sermon has been encouraging people to put things into the perspective of heaven, to be mindful that our Creator has given to us a life that is broader and bigger then we presently imagine. You would expect that religious ritual—sacrifice and worship—designed to reinforce those perceptions of the bigness of life, would be valued and encouraged above all else. But this is not the case: "So if you are offering your gift at the altar, and there remember that your brother has something against you, leave your gift there before the altar and go; first be reconciled to your brother, and then come and offer your gift" (5:23-24).

Instead, we are encouraged to not allow even religion to stand in the way of maintaining good interpersonal relationships. It's not that the sacrifice or religious ritual is bad. It's simply that ritual isn't a valid substitute for living out the values of heaven. It's hypocritical and, we might suspect, liable to the same criticism leveled by Isaiah:

> Bring no more vain offerings;
> incense is an abomination to me.
> New moon and sabbath and the calling of assemblies—
> I cannot endure iniquity and solemn assembly.
> Your new moons and your appointed feasts
> my soul hates;
> they have become a burden to me,
> I am weary of bearing them. (Isaiah 1:13-14)

And just as in the time of Isaiah, the offering of the sacrifice here in Matthew was encouraged after things were made right with the other person. It may well be that only then, after enjoying a repaired friendship, that sacrifice is appropriate—there's more to be thankful for, and the ritual can become an authentic expression of the joy of heaven. The point is that the other person is important, and no amount of religious devotion will replace genuine human care. Hope won't allow it.

Sexual lust and marital faithfulness are also touched by the values of heaven. Lust is antithetical to the values of heaven, for it reduces its object to nothing more than a thing (a tool, really) that has no value other than giving pleasure to someone else. Lust robs its object of their personhood and so makes no sense where heaven is concerned. Likewise, Jesus' statement about marriage is aimed at placing a high value on another person: "It was also said, 'Whoever divorces his wife, let him give her a certificate of divorce.' But I say to you that every one who divorces his wife, except on the ground of unchastity, makes her an adulteress; and whoever marries a divorced woman commits adultery" (Matthew 5:31-32).

Unfortunately, this part of the Sermon on the Mount has been used in attempts to distinguish valid circumstances for divorce from those that Jesus considered invalid. But that misses the mark altogether. The whole point of this statement is to show how important it is to be faithful, especially to the person with whom you have promised to walk through life. Whether granted a certificate or not, think hard before you break your promise—it can have devastating consequences on another person, and he or she deserves better. And this type of disruption has a ripple effect. Not only is the spouse harmed by a broken promise, but that person's future partner is affected too. Keeping your word is an important way in which hope becomes contagious. It's just what people who believe in heaven do.

That same theme of valuing people runs through the last excerpt from this part of the Sermon:

> Do not resist one who is evil. But if any one strikes you on the right cheek, turn to him the other also; and if any one would sue you and take your coat, let him have your cloak as well; and if any one forces you to go one mile, go with him two miles. Give to him who begs from you, and do not refuse him who would borrow from you.... But I say to you, Love your enemies and pray for those who persecute you, so that you may be sons of your Father who is in heaven; for he makes his sun rise on the evil and on the good, and sends rain on the just and on the unjust. For if you love those who love you, what reward have you?
>
> (5:39-42, 44-46a)

Being kind and generous, even to the point of being taken advantage of, makes sense only if people are more important than the possessions they want to take. And extending love to an enemy—to someone who has already done harm or injury—is simply ludicrous unless there is more to come. It makes no sense at all, as long as life is defined by the here and now. But if there is more, if heaven is a future promised by God, then living according to the norms of that reality doesn't sound like such a bad idea. A reward for this extraordinary behavior is alluded to in Matthew 5:46—"For if you love those who love you, what reward have you?"—and I'll be honest, I can't imagine what that reward might look like. But this much is sure: Loving people and valuing other people above everything else is a behavior we learn by imitating the Father. For if nothing else, the Creator has certainly modeled the fact that people matter.

When You Pray (Matthew 6:9-13)

Called by different names—the "Our Father" or the "Lord's Prayer"—these five verses are probably the best known verses in the entire Bible:

> Our Father who art in heaven,
> Hallowed be thy name.
> Thy kingdom come.
> Thy will be done,
>   On earth as it is in heaven.
> Give us this day our daily bread;
> And forgive us our debts,
>   As we also have forgiven our debtors;
> And lead us not into temptation,
>   But deliver us from evil. (Matthew 6:9-13)

In my mind, this is the hardest part of the entire Sermon on the Mount, and the very crux of the matter for us: "Thy kingdom come. / Thy will be done, / on earth as it is in heaven" (verse 10).

This is a dangerous prayer. It will not be tamed, though many have tried often enough. I've been in situations where the prayer has been used almost as magic to secure God's approval for decisions already made. I've watched as politicians and military leaders have used the prayer as a sort of cloak of protection prior to a military engagement. I've seen the prayer used by religious officials who were simply using the prayer to publicly proclaim their own piety, with an intent to reassert their own position of social prominence. In all of these, the prayer was being used as an attempt to bring the power of heaven to earth, not as a replacement for the earthly kingdoms, but simply to affirm the kingdoms of earth.

In reality, this is a prayer for an invasion. It's a prayer that heaven invade earth. It is a prayer that the kingdom of earth be overrun and undone. Implicit in the prayer is the willingness of the one mouthing these words to be involved in the invasion. Not involved through violence and the exercise of power, but through peacemaking and meekness, through pursuing righteousness, and by being merciful and pure in heart. This invasion may involve grief and poverty. And it certainly is characterized by forgiveness.

This invasion by heaven is serious business and should be prayed only by those who have counted the cost. It should be prayed only by those willing to live heaven's values. But if our goal is finding heaven, then it only makes sense that we be willing agents of heaven's appearing. Think twice before you pray these words. God may just answer your prayer, and it might not be what you expect.

I recently was on the receiving end of a prayer answered. One of the joys of being a college professor is the wide variety of fascinating students with whom you get to interact. They are at a stage when their lives are changing rapidly; and for a while, at least, they let you in on some of the transformations. Often, I think they make a much bigger impact on me then I could ever hope to make on them.

One afternoon, after classes were over for the day, I was sitting in my office working on some project or other when I heard a soft knock at the door. I opened it, and standing there was a student who was enrolled in one of the classes I was teaching that semester. He had in his hands a large book. The student held the book out and said, "Here, this is for you." We had just finished Matthew's Gospel in class, and what he handed to me was a copy of the Sermon on the Mount, illustrated with wonderful lithographic drawings. At that point, he wasn't aware of my special interest in the Sermon and the role model that it was providing for me; and so I was, in C. S. Lewis's words, "surprised by joy." I have the book open in front of me now. The page with the Lord's Prayer on it has a drawing of angels in heaven, leaning over and watching a shower of precious stones and gems falling down, figuratively describing heaven's invasion of earth contained in the prayer.

Inked inside the front cover of the book is the handwritten name of a woman, *Annie*, with the date under it, *July 24, 1891.* I've often wondered about Annie—what kind of person she was, and if she too was in search of a guide to heaven. But what has struck me is the way in which her name will now forever, in my mind at least, be associated with the Sermon on the Mount, and with this prayer in particular. Annie plainly made her name identified with the hope of heaven.

That's how it is with people who are courageous enough to pray this prayer. They, too, are staking their identities on a reality yet to come. They want heaven to come. Everything depends upon it.

Where Your Treasure Is (Matthew 6:19–7:27)

> Do not lay up for yourselves treasures on earth, where moth and rust consume and where thieves break in and steal, but lay up for yourselves treasures in heaven, where neither moth nor rust consumes and where thieves do not break in and steal. For where your treasure is, there will your heart be also. (Matthew 6:19-21)

The last part of the Sermon gets to the matters of life. It makes the reader consider the source of life's necessities upon which we are dependent. Food, clothes, a place to stay; where do these things come from, and how do we go about satisfying our need for the basics of life? For that matter, where exactly does our dependency lie?

In answer to these questions, the Sermon, in not-so-subtle a fashion, directs us to heaven: "But seek first [God's] kingdom and his righteousness, and all these things shall be yours as well" (6:33).

And illustrations of this are all around. Repeatedly, the Sermon points out example after example of God's care for what he has created:

> Look at the birds of the air; they neither sow nor reap nor gather into barns, and yet your heavenly Father feeds them. Are you not of more value than they? ... Consider the lilies of the field, how they grow; they neither toil nor spin; yet I tell you, even Solomon in all his glory was not clothed like one of these. But if God so clothes the grass of the field ... will he not much more clothe you—you of little faith? (6:26, 28-30, NRSV)

> Ask, and it will be given you; seek, and you will find; knock, and it will be opened to you. ... If you then, who are evil, know how to give good gifts to your children, how much more will your Father who is in heaven give good things to those who ask him! (7:7, 11)

Given the care that God so obviously showers upon the works of his hands—care that we can see all around us—how can we think that we should receive anything less? There is a remarkable freedom here. Free from the fear of death and confident in the hope of heaven, we are free to pursue heaven with reckless abandon.

But even this reckless abandon in pursuit of heaven has been twisted and perverted to become something other than what the Creator intended. Some have altered, distorted, and misused this freedom, marked it by death and destruction. But this isn't the freedom that the Sermon has in mind at all. This freedom isn't marked by terror, but it is a freedom to pursue a lifestyle marked out by the Beatitudes. The reckless abandon that Jesus advocated isn't the occasion of terror and hatred, but just the opposite: "Judge not, that you be not judged. For with the judgment you pronounce you will be judged, and the measure you give will be the measure you get" (7:1-2).

Narrow the Gate

This is what a lifestyle looks like for those who truly believe in heaven. It's a lifestyle that values people. It is meek and peace-loving. A life lived with heaven in mind understands that our possessions are temporary and fading away, never the source of a security we can find only in God. The Sermon is the role model for a life lived with heaven in mind. It seems so simple—on paper. Living it out is quite another thing, and it is no harder now then it was in Jesus' own day. Jesus recognized the difficulty of living the path to heaven: "Enter by the narrow gate; for the gate is wide and the way is easy, that leads to destruction, and those who enter by it are many. For the gate is narrow and the way is hard, that leads to life, and those who find it are few" (7:13-14).

To make matters worse, not everyone who claims to offer a map for the way is a reliable guide. For immediately after these words about a narrow and presumably hard-to-find gate, we read that you even need to be careful about those who would offer you direction along the way. It's a bit ironic that right smack dab in the middle of a discussion about finding heaven, we have a warning against "false prophets" (7:15).

How, then, are we to know who is giving good directions from those who would sell to us their bad advice? Jesus returns us to the test that we borrowed from him back at the beginning of this book: "You will know them by their fruits" (7:16). In other words, *Does it work? Does the advice make you more functional? Or does the information you receive, from whatever source, simply support a religious system or other social institution?* These questions can't honestly be answered until you take the first step. But that's the hardest part, isn't it? I wish I knew of a way to make it easier, but I don't. I don't know what may wait for you. I suspect that, like mine, your journey will be filled with the wonderful and the tragic. What I can confidently tell you is that the journey is definitely worth the risk.

And so, now it's time to put it to the test. The Creator has guaranteed you a life beyond the grave. Listening to the God-echo deep within can produce a hope of heaven accompanied by joy and peace. The delight God takes in you, the work of his hands, will not be frustrated by the grave. It is now time to put the guide aside and begin the journey.

EPILOGUE

MARTIN HEIDEGGER, A PROMINENT philosopher of the twentieth century, declared that being human is "being-towards-death." By that phrase, he meant that the grave is waiting for us all, and we know it (*Being and Time*, translated by John Macquarrie and Edward Robinson; Harper and Row, 1962; pages 279–96). So the best we can do is live today to the fullest. Jesus, too, recognized the reality of death but turned it on its head: "Jesus said to her, 'I am the resurrection and the life. Those who believe in me, even though they die, will live, and everyone who lives and believes in me will never die'" (John 11:25-26a, NRSV).

According to Jesus, to be human, at least truly human, is not to be toward death, but to be toward life. Being toward life, that's the promise of hope given to us by the Creator. That hope is the echo of a home forgotten, a God-echo that calls us onward. It's a hope that resonates deeply within us all, providing a sense of confidence in things that are yet unseen.

The words of 1 Corinthians ring true: "For now we see in a mirror dimly, but then face to face. Now I know in part; then I shall understand fully, even as I have been fully understood" (13:12).

One of the most amazing things I have discovered in my quest of heaven is that the journey begins now. Heaven isn't just for later when I die. Instead, glimpses of heaven invade the present, making me different and causing me to see everything else in a new light. This has had a deep effect on me. In many ways, I feel like my life has just begun. I've learned that this doubt—doubt about heaven—is not resolved through the addition of more information only, but it is resolved fundamentally by trust. Trust in the Creator and trust in his goodness.

My quest began in response to my wife's question: "Do I have a future?" I wanted to answer her honestly, and at last, I think I can. Yes. Yes, Cher, you do have a future. There is a green and fair country waiting for you. One for which you were made, and one promised by the Creator himself. And I will meet you there.

> He will wipe away every tear from their eyes, and death shall be no more, neither shall there be mourning nor crying nor pain any more, for the former things have passed away. (Revelation 21:4)

SELECT BIBLIOGRAPHY

A READER FAMILIAR WITH SOME of the current scholarship on the Old Testament will recognize immediately a variety of influences present in this book. I make no claim to originality. In fact, such a claim would probably be a sign that the book is of little value. The writers and books listed below are, in my mind, especially worth reading.

Brueggemann, Walter, *An Introduction to the Old Testament: The Canon and Christian Imagination* (Westminster John Knox Press, 2003).

Crenshaw, James L., *Old Testament Wisdom: An Introduction* (Westminster John Knox Press, 1998).

Lewis, C. S., *Mere Christianity* (Macmillan, 1952).

Westermann, Claus, *Elements of Old Testament Theology* (Westminster John Knox Press, 1982).

Wolff, Hans Walter, *Anthropology of the Old Testament* (Fortress Press, 1974).

Yount, David, *What Are We to Do? Living the Sermon on the Mount* (Sheed and Ward, 2002).

Zimmerli, Walther, *Man and His Hope in the Old Testament* (SCM Press, 1971). This is a wonderful book, even if a bit on the academic side. The structure of Part Two of *A Doubter's Guide to Heaven* is especially indebted to Zimmerli's work.

DISCUSSION GUIDE FOR
A DOUBTER'S GUIDE TO HEAVEN

Pamela Dilmore

Chapter 1
The Crisis: A Journey Begins

1. The author's wife was diagnosed with cancer, which made him seek answers about the "ugly specter of death." When has a personal crisis led you to seek answers about death? What happened? What was it like?
2. The author's statement, "We have cancer," indicates a deep empathy with his wife. How do personal crises affect your close personal relationships? Do you draw closer? withdraw? Why?
3. The author's quest began a spiritual journey. He questioned everything he thought he ever knew or believed about God, the spiritual life, and eternity. He wanted and needed hope. What events in your life have led you on a spiritual journey? What was it like for you?

Chapter 2
Do I Have a Future?

1. The author shared that serious, personal conversation with those close to him became much more important to him when his wife was diagnosed with a serious illness. Why do you think this occurred? Have you had a similar experience? If so, what became important to you?

2. Late one night the author's wife asked, "Do I have a future?" How would you respond to this question?

3. The author indicated that options after death were "either heaven or oblivion, and oblivion was an unthinkable prospect." He equated *hell* and *oblivion*, and he decided that his quest was involved with heaven. How do you respond to his view of the options?

4. The author and a colleague wondered whether or not much of their academic work was really an effort to avoid the question, "Does heaven really exist?" Reading books and listening to sermons became inadequate. The author began to question sources upon which he had formerly relied. His question became, "Is guidance available, and can a reliable guide be found? Is there a map for the journey?" What are your questions about heaven?

Chapter 3
A Map for the Journey

1. What does the phrase "a fork in the road" suggest to you? How do you respond to Yogi Berra's saying about a fork in the road? What do you do when you come to a fork in the road?

2. How do you respond to the author's point of view about the authority of religious professionals as a map for understanding heaven? By what criteria do you judge religious professionals?

3. How do you respond to the author's perspectives regarding the Bible as the map for understanding heaven?

4. The author quotes Jesus as a way to determine the value of an authority, whether that authority is a person or a book: "By their fruits you will know them." How do you respond to this as a guideline for doubters?

5. The author finds hope in the "deeply-embedded awareness" of the eternal that is part of all human existence. He asserts that our beliefs "can either be in concert or in disharmony"

with this God-given awareness. He believes that we function best when our beliefs are in concert with our awareness of the eternal. Do you experience such awareness? What is it like? How does it shape what you believe?

Chapter 4
God Tucked Me In

1. The author describes a comforting sense of God's presence at a moment of great despair after his wife's surgery. When have you felt a similar experience of God's comforting presence? What was it like?
2. The author's experience of being "tucked in" by God led to his discovery of new meaning in the image of the loving father in Psalm 103. When has your personal experience given deeper meaning to Scripture? Which Scripture passages became "functional" for you as a result?
3. The author describes a view of heaven as "fully realizing the closeness of God." How do you respond to his description? What is your view of heaven?
4. Read Luke 17:20-21. How do you respond to this Scripture passage? How do the words "the kingdom of God is in the midst of you" speak to you?

Chapter 5
Moriah

1. When, if ever, have you had doubts about God? What was it like? What kinds of questions emerged from your doubt?
2. Read Genesis 22 about Abraham responding to God's instruction to sacrifice his son Isaac. How do you respond to this story? What questions does it raise for you?
3. Genesis 22 offered a ray of hope to the author, a hope reflected in his poem. How do you respond to the poem? How do you see hope offered on Mount Moriah?

4. The author's experience in dealing with his wife's cancer led him to realize that all his previous ways of understanding God were being shattered. Have you ever had an experience like this? What was it like?

Chapter 6
A Good God?

1. In the opening paragraph, the author asks, "How can the love of God be reconciled with something like a devastating illness, separation, and death?" How do you respond to this question?
2. The author describes confusion and rage toward God as he thought about horrendous loss of life in events such as the tsunami in Southeast Asia, war in Iraq, and the suffering of children in parts of Africa. Have you ever been confused and angry with God? What prompted your feelings? What was it like for you?
3. The author found resolution to his anger and a sense of overwhelming joy when he realized that love was at the heart of his experience. He says that God, out of love, created the universe in which we can choose to love and to experience love, and that our rejection of love leads to pain and harm for ourselves and others. Do you agree or disagree? Why?
4. The author says, "The very fact of the pain, heartache, and terrible grief that death and suffering bring is evidence that disease, tragedy, and death are not the way things ought to be; we weren't created to find fulfillment with them. These things do bother us because they are contrary to the way we were made. Something went wrong, and love was rejected." How do you respond to this view? The author asks, "The question is, can it be fixed? Can love be made the norm?" How do you answer his question?

Chapter 7
A Vision of Hope in the Wisdom Literature

1. How do you define *hope*? How important is hope in our lives?
2. Read Proverbs 11:23: "The desire of the righteous ends only in good; / the expectation of the wicked in wrath." What, if anything, challenges you about this verse? Do you believe its claim? Why or why not? Read Proverbs 23:17-18: "Let not your heart envy sinners, / but continue in the fear of the LORD all the day. / Surely there is a future, / and your hope will not be cut off." How do you respond to these verses? How are these two passages of Scripture the same? How are they different? How do they speak about hope?
3. The author states, "Ultimately, it is not the future or things promised in the future upon which hope rests. Instead, hope rests in God himself (Proverbs 14:26; 22:19)." How do you respond to his insight?
4. The author points out that Job "finds himself in a situation in which all hope has been removed." Job does not refuse to believe or turn his back on God; rather, Job believes that God has turned his back on him and taken hope with him. The author says, "Job can't conjure up hope, nor can he produce hope by wishing it or piously living it." When have you felt like Job? What was it like for you? What conclusions did you make from your situation?
5. The author says, "Job's friends were attempting to argue the right to hope based upon a person's moral character—that is, God is bound to act beneficially in the future based upon the integrity of the person today. But Job will have nothing to do with this argument. Instead, he argues that hope is assured, not because of anything he has done, but simply on the basis that God has created, and that God will not abandon his creation. It is in God alone, and in his past and evident acts of creation, that hope is

assured." How do you respond to these remarks, to the different arguments put forth by Job and his friends?

Chapter 8
A Vision of Hope in the Psalms

1. In the opening paragraph the author asserts that doubts about heaven are ultimately doubts about God. Do you agree or disagree with this assertion? Why? Explain.
2. Read Psalm 1. How do you respond to the notion that hope belongs to the righteous and is withheld from the unrighteous? How does this idea play out in your life experience? How does the idea that the future belongs to God affect your thinking about this moral basis for hope?
3. Read Psalm 37:9, 34, which present the admonition to "wait for the LORD." The author describes this waiting as an attitude of complete openness to the God. How does such an attitude relate to hope for the future? How does it help us "function" from day to day?
4. Read Psalm 119:49-50, 74, 114, 147. The author says, "The word of God that gives guidance and help for the present is also able to provide security and comfort— hope for the future." Further he says, "Hope is found only in God; yet there is a sense in which that hope is expressed through the lives of those who recognize their dependency upon the LORD." Psalm 119 communicates this recognition. How do you see this reliance upon the witness of others, as described in the psalm, as a basis for hope in your life?
5. Read Psalm 39. How do despair and lament lead us to hope in God?

Chapter 9
A Vision of Hope in the Torah

1. The author says in the opening paragraph, "Hope is a byproduct of . . . living life in the presence of God." Do you agree or disagree with this statement? Explain your response.
2. How do you find hope in the stories of God creating the world and human beings in Genesis 1 and 2? How do you find hope in the story of the Fall in Genesis 3? How do you see hope in the story of Cain and Abel in Genesis 4? in the story of Noah and the Flood in Genesis 6–8?
3. In response to God's promise to Jacob in Genesis 28:13-14, the author says, "Hope is present, not just for Abraham and his family, but hope is near for all the families of the earth. Consistently in all these dealings between God and the family of Abraham, the real goal is a blessing applied to all humanity." In view of the trouble and tragedy in our world, how do you see this blessing at work today?
4. After reading about all the different names for God and what they say about hope, how would you name God?
5. Read Isaiah 40:28-31. What speaks most to you in this Scripture? How does it communicate hope?

Chapter 10
Heaven Is Where You Are

1. The author's recollections of a war-torn city are graphic and heartbreaking. He describes violence, destruction, and disease. How do you respond to the scenes he describes?
2. How do you think anyone could find hope in the scenes the author describes?
3. The author describes a visit to the home of a friend and conversations in a coffee shop of sorts as some of his best memories of human kindness amidst the despair and

violence. When have you or someone you know experienced human kindness in tragic situations? What was it like? How was God present?

4. Going home and seeing his wife was key to the author's hope. He used it as a way to express "the presence of God that makes heaven special." How does going home or seeing someone you love express the hope of heaven to you?

5. The author asks, "Could it be that there is actually the possibility that I can experience heaven now, and that *experience* is the very best proof that there is more to come?" How would you answer him?

Chapter 11
Neither Here nor There

1. The author opens the chapter with this statement: "Doubt results when the old paradigms, the old ways of looking at things, simply don't work any longer. For me, personal crisis convinced me that my old way of looking at things—and my way of looking at God, in particular—simply wouldn't do." Have you ever had this kind of experience? What was it like? Where did it lead you?

2. How do you understand "religion" and "spirituality"? Are the two different for you? Explain.

3. How do our perceptions of where we are affect our views of God? How do our understandings of the universe affect our views of God? How do these views affect our understandings of heaven?

4. The author says, "We live in a world in which neither here nor there matters anymore. Distance, space, and location are being erased in two seemingly contradictory ways.... The Internet and its corollary communication technologies have effectively erased the distance between people so that 'there' has lost much of its meaning in human discourse." How do you respond to this assertion by the author?

5. The author asks: "What is heaven like in a world where 'here' and 'there' have little meaning?" How would you answer his question? How do you respond to his idea that heaven is a way of being rather than a place?

Chapter 12
I Looked Through the Keyhole

1. The author asks: "Does a taste of heaven *now* awaken in us a longing that, in turn, provides evidence of more to come?" How do you respond to this question?
2. When the author asked his wife why she was so confident about heaven, she responded, "I looked through the keyhole." She described looking through the keyhole of the door to heaven as experiencing an overwhelming joy for which there was no immediate or explainable cause. Have you had such moments? What were they like? How would you describe "looking through the keyhole" of the door to heaven?
3. Read Romans 15:13. What is the source of joy here? How do you see the God of hope as the source of joy and peace in your life?
4. How might the joy of believing affect our way of life now, on a day-to-day basis?
5. The author says, "Love and grief are partners in a lifelong dance." How do you respond to his assertion? Is it true for you? How?

Chapter 13
A Search for a Role Model

1. How do you respond to the idea that searching for answers about what heaven is like, or how heaven makes a difference in life, is a lonely quest?
2. Have you or someone you know had deep questions about heaven? about resurrection? How do people in

your church, in your discussion group, in your family, or in your close circle of friends respond to the expression of such doubts?

3. Read Matthew 5–7. How does the Sermon on the Mount help you think about heaven? How might it guide your journey to heaven?

4. What does it mean to you to understand God's kingdom as here and now? as a destination at some point in our future? How does the author's admonition to "live with heaven in mind" resonate with you?